Navigating the Journey in Budgeting

Navigating the Journey in Budgeting

Major Steps in Making a Complex Subject Manageable

Christopher Ursu

ROWMAN & LITTLEFIELD
Lanham • Boulder • New York • London

Published by Rowman & Littlefield
An imprint of The Rowman & Littlefield Publishing Group, Inc.

4501 Forbes Boulevard, Suite 200, Lanham, Maryland 20706

www.rowman.com

86-90 Paul Street, London EC2A 4NE, United Kingdom

Copyright © 2023 by Christopher Ursu

All figures created by author.

All rights reserved. No part of this book may be reproduced in any form or by any electronic or mechanical means, including information storage and retrieval systems, without written permission from the publisher, except by a reviewer who may quote passages in a review.

British Library Cataloguing in Publication Information Available

Library of Congress Cataloging-in-Publication Data

Names: Ursu, Christopher, 1973– author.
Title: Navigating the journey in budgeting : major steps in making a complex subject manageable / Christopher Ursu.
Description: Lanham : Rowman & Littlefield, [2023] | Summary: "The book explains the general applications of a budget and budgeting principles and methods"—Provided by publisher.
Identifiers: LCCN 2023001876 (print) | LCCN 2023001877 (ebook) | ISBN 9781475866513 (cloth) | ISBN 9781475866520 (paperback) | ISBN 9781475866537 (epub)
Subjects: LCSH: School budgets. | School districts—Finance.
Classification: LCC LB2830 .U78 2023 (print) | LCC LB2830 (ebook) | DDC 371.2/06—dc23/eng/20230310
LC record available at https://lccn.loc.gov/2023001876
LC ebook record available at https://lccn.loc.gov/2023001877

Contents

Foreword	vii
Preface	ix
Acknowledgments	xi
Introduction	xiii
Chapter 1: Budget Applications	1
Chapter 2: Statistical Measures and Methods	9
Chapter 3: School District Operations and Expenses	15
Chapter 4: Budgeting School District Expenses	29
Chapter 5: Budgeting School District Revenues	37
Chapter 6: The Budget Layout	45
Chapter 7: The Budgeting Process	57
Chapter 8: Small Town School District	61
Chapter 9: Stage 1: Establish Goals, Parameters, and Plans	71
Chapter 10: Stage 2: Develop the Personnel Budget	77
Chapter 11: Stage 3: Develop the Non-Personnel Budget	85
Chapter 12: Stage 4: Budget Miscellaneous Expenses and Add Contingency Allowance	97
Chapter 13: Stage 5: Budget Revenues	107
Chapter 14: Stage 6: Meet, Make Adjustments, and Finalize Budget	113

Index 125

About the Author 129

Foreword

I met Chris Ursu several years ago through membership and networking within the school business official's association. Chris quickly became not only a valued colleague, but a trusted friend as well. We immediately connected over our interest in developing and improving the practices of the school business profession.

During my forty-two years serving as and supporting school business officials, I have seen a plethora of various school budgeting processes and practices. Some of those have served to provide some level of success and many others have been less than efficient and effective. The issue seems to be that there is a lack of resources and training available to assist and provide guidance to the school administrative staff with budget processes that work effectively in a school district setting. In other words, there are limited references that provide specific guidance on budgeting techniques that serve to support the mission of the school district. So often, the processes are carried forward from year to year and are not reviewed for efficiency and effectiveness. A comprehensive and valuable budget process that is established and followed assures that resources are properly allocated, that all stakeholders have input, and that budget decisions are supported with appropriate data and rationale.

Navigating the Journey in Budgeting is a refreshing and much needed resource to help districts review, establish, and/or adjust their current budget practices. School district budgeting is as much an art as it is a science and needs to be viewed from those lenses. Traditionally, the school business official has been more comfortable with the science piece of it, due to the nature of those in these particular positions. Their personality, background, experience, and education tend to support a more "scientific" approach. No matter the experience and level of comfort, every school and its staff will benefit by reading this book and reflecting on school district budgeting. School district budgeting is unique and unlike budgeting for any other organization. As such, it is a subject that deserves its own dedicated resource to deal with the distinctiveness of school budget development.

Chris is uniquely qualified to evaluate school budgeting practices with a distinct perspective relative to his experience inside and outside of education. He has an undergraduate degree in engineering, an MBA, and has had work experience in the field of engineering and banking prior to his move to school business administration. School budgeting is complex and challenging. It takes a great deal of skill to navigate the various and numerous needs and wants of the stakeholders. Balancing needs and wants with available resources, which are often very limited, is challenging at best. Budgeting for schools must be done with great care, with acknowledgment of the crucial impact it has on our future generations. Chris understands and embraces the importance of a best practice process. The bottom line is that improvement in budgeting practices and adherence to Chris's recommendations, results in a positive impact on the lives of the children and families that school districts serve.

This book outlines and provides detail on the budgeting process from beginning to end. Chris provides guidance on budget applications, styles, and forecasting methods. He outlines the budget process and provides specific direction on both the technical and non-technical aspects of school budgeting. Chris's expertise is evident as he shares best practice through the various lenses of his education, background, and many years of experience in both school administration and banking. If you are involved at any level in school district budgeting, you need to read this book. There is much to gain from his insights and guidance in this helpful and valuable resource.

Stan H. Wisler, MBA
PA Certified School Business Official
Author of *Words Matter: Embracing the Power of Conversation*

Preface

I began my career in school business management with a school district that had been without a business administrator for several months. The business office support staff had kept essential functions—like the processing of payroll and the payment of bills—flowing, but activities relating to financial management and planning had been neglected. This presented a major challenge, particularly because I had never worked in a school district setting and would have to present the following year's budget in a matter of months.

I knew I had to learn as much as I could, as quickly as possible, about school operations and finances. Unfortunately, there was no training manual available, so I began by meeting with coworkers so that I could ask questions and gain knowledge from them. I also joined the countywide school business administrators' networking group and the Pennsylvania Association of School Business Officials, which offered training seminars on various aspects of school budgeting. When I was not attending meetings or seminars, I studied the district's business records, audit report, and most recent budget to familiarize myself with its finances. Through this rather haphazard process, I was somehow able to gain enough understanding to develop and present the budget on time.

In the years since that experience, I have developed a much greater understanding of school districts and the complexities and challenges of school budgeting. Using a process largely consisting of trial and error, I have developed and honed a set of efficient and effective procedures to create a school budget. I wrote this book to share the knowledge and insights I have gained about school operations and budgeting and to document the budgeting practices I now use. The book provides a road map for those interested in learning about school budgeting, breaking down an otherwise complex process into a series of manageable steps.

Various groups will benefit by reading this book. School business administrators who are new to the profession can use it to accelerate their learning and avoid missteps, while seasoned veterans can use it as a source for new ideas and approaches. Superintendents, school boards, and other district leaders can use it to improve their understanding of budgeting principles and practices. The book is also intended for use in college courses for students pursuing careers in public administration, business administration, or finance.

Acknowledgments

I would first like to thank my parents and grandparents for their love, support, and guidance. They always made sure that humor was a part of my life and instilled in me an understanding of the importance of education and perseverance.

I would next like to thank my wife and kids, who amaze me every day. They give my life meaning and have been so supportive as I have taken on the challenge of writing a book.

I would also like to thank my sister. We have been through a lot together, and she has always been there for me.

I would like to thank my numerous aunts, uncles, and cousins as well. I am lucky to be part of such a close-knit family.

I would like to give special thanks to Stan Wisler, author of *Words Matter: Embracing the Power of Conversation*. After attending a webinar at which Stan spoke, I contacted him to ask about his experience as a writer, and he quickly became a good friend and mentor.

Finally, I would like to thank the many teachers and work colleagues I have met and learned from over the years. The knowledge and insight they have shared have helped me to become the person I am today.

Introduction

As local education agencies, school districts are charged with educating students, equipping them with the knowledge and skills they will need as adults to be productive members of society. This goal is accomplished by providing an array of instructional and related services. To ensure that adequate resources are available for these services, a financial plan, or budget, must be in place. This book offers a road map for developing a school district budget by providing an overview of general budgeting applications, concepts, and techniques; a background in school district operations and finances; and a set of recommended procedures to take the budget from inception to completion.

Chapter 1 begins by explaining the relationship between revenues, expenses, and financial position before exploring the applications of a budget in managing financial position through planning, control, and assessment. The importance of budget accuracy to all three of these functions is explained, and the drawbacks of overly aggressive or cautious budgeting styles are illustrated using simple household and business budgets as examples. The chapter concludes with an explanation of how to account for risk through use of a contingency allowance.

Chapter 2 analyzes a set of hypothetical costs using statistical techniques to demonstrate how these techniques can be used to make budget forecasts. Two measures that are used to express the central value in a data set (mean and median) and two that are used to account for data trends (average annual change and average percentage change) are discussed. The chapter concludes with a review of more advanced forecasting methods known as regression analyses.

Chapter 3 shifts away from general budgeting applications and techniques to focus on school districts, describing their programs and operations, the resources they require, and the costs entailed. The discussion covers both regular and special education programs; instructional support functions such as nursing, guidance, and psychological services; and ancillary student services such as extracurricular programs and transportation. The administration and management of these programs is also covered.

Next, plant operations—encompassing the maintenance and care of buildings, equipment, and grounds—are reviewed, followed by an overview of technology operations and network components. The roles and responsibilities of a district's business office, central office, board of directors, and public relations personnel are also explained. The chapter concludes with a more thorough examination of personnel and supplies expenses.

Chapter 4 explains how to project various types of school district expenses, beginning with employee compensation. Employee salaries are considered first, with a primary focus on teacher salaries. Employee wages are considered next, including both regular and overtime wages as well as the budgeting of substitute costs. Next, the discussion turns to budgeting common employee benefits before delving into the budgeting of common non-personnel costs such as loan and lease payments, contracted services, and supplies.

Chapter 5 explains how to project various types of local, state, and federal revenues. Local revenues are considered first, focusing primarily on property taxes, often the most significant source of local revenue. The interrelationship between the tax base, rate, and collection percentage in calculating tax revenues is explained, and other forms of local revenue, such as investment income and local grants, are also considered. The budgeting of state and federal revenues is discussed in the second half of the chapter.

Chapter 6 deals with the overall organization of the budget, recommending that expense accounts be grouped by functional area and revenue accounts be classified as either local, state, or federal. Two types of expense accounts are recommended: those to record planned costs that can be tied to specific employees or items during budget planning and those to record spontaneous spending that cannot be tied to specific sources ahead of time. (The recommendations in this and subsequent chapters assume the absence of a feature in some accounting systems that allows costs to be charged before any obligation to make payment exists.)

The recommended format also includes two budgets that are subsidiary to the main expenditure budget: one that is used to project personnel expenses associated with specific employees (subsidiary personnel budget) and another that is used to project non-personnel costs associated with specific items (subsidiary non-personnel budget).

Chapter 7 touches on the ongoing nature of certain aspects of school district budgeting and suggests ways to carry out this work efficiently. The chapter discussion concludes by breaking the budgeting process down into six major stages and explaining how the chapters that follow relate to those stages.

Chapter 8 provides a detailed description of a hypothetical school district that is used in subsequent chapters to demonstrate the application of the budgeting procedures described and recommended in each chapter.

Chapter 9 recommends a process for school boards to use, with the assistance of district administrators, to establish strategic goals and parameters to guide the development of the budget. Suggested steps for district administrators to use in developing plans to achieve those goals within the stipulated parameters are also outlined.

Chapter 10 details steps that can be used to develop an initial version of the subsidiary personnel budget, which is then linked to the main expenditure budget. The chapter includes a recommendation to highlight budget estimates that may be adjusted later and to assign a priority level to each position.

Chapter 11 outlines procedures for developing an initial version of the subsidiary non-personnel budget, a major aspect of which is to solicit and enter purchase requests from employees for the upcoming year. The collaborative nature of the budgeting process is also discussed.

Chapter 12 pertains to the budgeting of expenses for employees or items that cannot be identified in advance during budget planning. A recommendation is made to budget these costs directly in the main expenditure budget in accounts designated to record this type of spending only. The addition of a contingency allowance to the overall budget is also demonstrated in this chapter.

Chapter 13 begins with a review of the concepts presented on local revenues in chapter 5. The revenue budget development process is then broken down into two major steps, and the hypothetical school district introduced in chapter 8 is used to illustrate the application of those steps. This illustration is also used to demonstrate how grant revenue and expenditure budgets are related.

Chapter 14 begins with a quick recap of concepts from chapters 10–12 pertaining to the budgeting of expenses. Steps to complete the budgeting process are then recommended and explained, which in summary include:

- furnishing budget reports to administrators or managers
- holding meetings to discuss recommended changes
- adjusting the budget and checking the results
- presenting the budget
- performing remaining administrative tasks

Chapter 1

Budget Applications

A budget is a tool that is used to manage financial position by projecting revenues and expenses over a future time period, typically one year. Revenues cause financial position to increase, while expenses cause it to decrease. When budgeted revenues exceed expenses, the difference represents a projected surplus and equivalent increase in financial position. When expenses exceed revenues, it represents a projected deficit and equivalent decrease in financial position. When projected revenues equal projected expenses, no change in financial position is forecast.

Some revenue and expenditure projections are exact while others are estimates, and some expenditure projections are for required items while others are for discretionary items.

A budget is a tool for planning, control, and assessment. As it is developed, it is molded and adjusted to reflect and accommodate plans that are being formed. Once the budget is complete, it can be used as a control mechanism over spending by signaling when that spending is approaching budgetary limits. Budgets are also used to make ongoing assessments by comparing actual results to forecasts.

A budget must be reasonably accurate in order to serve as an effective tool. When plans are based on a realistic view of the future, expenses are controlled effectively through meaningful spending boundaries, and results are evaluated based on reasonable expectations.

PLANNING

A budget is formed based on future plans and is used to predict whether those plans are compatible with a desired financial outcome. When they are not, both the plans and the budget can be adjusted until the desired result is achieved.

Household Budget Example

The development and modification of a budget during planning can be illustrated using a simple household budget. Let's say an individual who wants to make a profit of $5,000 in the upcoming year initially develops the following budget:

Projected Revenues
- Job Salary: $48,000 (exact)
- Home Business Sales: $10,000 (estimate)
- Total Projected Revenues: $58,000

Projected Expenses from Required Items
- Fuel: $3,000 (estimate)
- Groceries: $4,800 (estimate)
- Insurance: $2,000 (exact)
- Rent: $13,400 (exact)
- Repairs: $2,000 (estimate)
- Utilities: $6,000 (estimate)
- Other Required Items: $12,000 (estimate)
- Total Projected Expenses from Required Items: $43,200

Projected Expenses from Discretionary Items
- Entertainment: $3,600 (estimate)
- Gym Membership: $1,200 (exact)
- Vacation: $6,000 (estimate)
- Total Projected Expenses from Discretionary Items: $10,800

Total Projected Expenses: $54,000
Projected Profit: $4,000

Since the goal is a profit of $5,000, the budget needs to be adjusted. Items to consider for revision are those labeled as discretionary. Options might be to (1) reduce the amount allocated for entertainment, (2) cancel the gym membership, or (3) take a cheaper vacation. If the third option is chosen, the modified budget might be as follows:

Projected Revenues
- Job Salary: $48,000 (exact)
- Home Business Sales: $10,000 (estimate)
- Total Projected Revenues: $58,000

Projected Expenses from Required Items
- Fuel: $3,000 (estimate)
- Groceries: $4,800 (estimate)
- Insurance: $2,000 (exact)

- Rent: $13,400 (exact)
- Repairs: $2,000 (estimate)
- Utilities: $6,000 (estimate)
- Other Required Items: $12,000 (estimate)
- Total Projected Expenses from Required Items: $43,200

Projected Expenses from Discretionary Items
- Entertainment: $3,600 (estimate)
- Gym Membership: $1,200 (exact)
- Vacation: $5,000 (estimate; reduced by $1,000)

Total Projected Expenses from Discretionary Items: $9,800 (reduced by $1,000)
Total Projected Expenses: $53,000 (reduced by $1,000)
Projected Profit: $5,000 (increased by $1,000)

By planning a cheaper vacation and adjusting the budget, the projected profit has been increased to the desired amount. (Note that another way to try to make up the difference between the projected and desired results is to look for ways to increase revenues.)

The Importance of Budget Accuracy to Planning

A budget's usefulness for planning is inextricably linked to its accuracy, or how close its projections are to actual results. An accurate budget provides reliable forecasts to decision makers so they can make wise choices. This is much like a weather forecast: If sunny skies are forecast, not taking an umbrella when venturing out will be a good decision as long as the forecast turns out to be accurate and a storm does not pass through.

As already mentioned, when budgets are created, some projections are exact while others are estimates. The way to achieve an accurate budget is to strive to make precise estimates through a moderate style that is neither overly aggressive (budgeting revenues on the high end and expenses on the low end) nor overly cautious (budgeting revenues on the low end and expenses on the high end).

In the example above, a decision was made to spend $9,800 on discretionary items because the budget indicated this would still allow for a profit of $5,000. If any of the estimates turn out to be highly inaccurate, though, things could go awry. Say, for example, that the home business generates $6,000 of sales instead of the budgeted amount of $10,000 and that the cost of utilities turns out to be $9,000 rather than the $6,000 that was projected. Assuming the remainder of the budget turns out to be accurate, the bottom line is a loss of $2,000 rather than the $5,000 profit that was forecast. Because the budget was too aggressive, poor decisions were made during the planning phase; discretionary expenses should have been limited to $2,800 rather than $9,800.

Budgeting more cautiously reduces the likelihood of overspending, but being too cautious has drawbacks of its own because it can lead to unnecessary spending cuts and missed opportunities. Returning to the example, a very cautious style used to generate the initial budget might result in the following:

Projected Revenues
- Job Salary: $48,000 (exact)
- Home Business Sales: $5,000 (estimate; $5,000 lower than in previous version)
- Total Projected Revenues: $53,000 ($5,000 lower than in previous version)

Projected Expenses from Required Items
- Fuel: $5,000 (estimate; $2,000 more than in previous version)
- Groceries: $6,000 (estimate; $1,200 more than in previous version)
- Insurance: $2,000 (exact)
- Rent: $13,400 (exact)
- Repairs: $4,000 (estimate; $2,000 more than in previous version)
- Utilities: $10,000 (estimate; $4,000 more than in previous version)
- Other Required Items: $12,000 (estimate)
- Total Projected Expenses from Required Items: $52,400 ($9,200 more than in previous version)

Projected Expenses from Discretionary Items
- Entertainment: $3,600 (estimate)
- Gym Membership: $1,200 (exact)
- Vacation: $5,000 (estimate)
- Total Projected Expenses from Discretionary Items: $9,800

Total Projected Expenses: $62,200 ($9,200 more than in previous version)
Projected Loss: –$9,200 ($14,200 less than in previous version)

Based on the bleaker forecast of the more cautious approach, a decision is made to cut the entire discretionary budget, eliminating all entertainment activities, canceling the gym membership, and forgoing a vacation in an effort to eke out a small profit. However, such extreme cuts were not necessary. The actual results indicate that up to $2,800 of discretionary spending could have been accommodated while earning a profit of $5,000.

CONTROL

A budget is a reflection of future plans. The budget projection indicates whether or not those plans are thought to be compatible with a desired financial outcome. Plans should be modified and the budget adjusted until the projection is satisfactory. Once it is finalized, the budget continues to act as a tool for safeguarding financial position by establishing financial boundaries within which spending choices can be made. Again, a simple household budget can be used to illustrate.

Assume a couple has budgeted $1,000 for their daughter to take small trips with friends while away at college and that the daughter is to obtain permission from her parents before taking any trips. Under this arrangement, her requests can be approved until her total spending reaches the budget limit of $1,000.

The Importance of Budget Accuracy to Control

As with planning, a budget's utility for control functions is dependent on its accuracy. When a budget is inaccurate because it has been developed using an overly aggressive style, it tends to set limits that are so restrictive they cannot accommodate spending that is normally needed. If the couple in the example above has budgeted $250 for car repairs but annual spending is typically closer to $1,000, it is quite likely the budgetary limit will be reached long before the year ends. The couple's only option at that point will be to forgo needed repairs or exceed the budget, neither of which is ideal.

A budget that is based on an overly cautious style also lacks usefulness as a control mechanism because its spending limits are so high that they never come into play. For instance, if the couple above has budgeted $20,000 for groceries that typically cost $600 per month, the budgetary amount is so far beyond what is needed that it will provide virtually no control whatsoever.

To summarize, budgetary limits must be relatively close to normal spending patterns (i.e., accurate) in order to provide meaningful control. A budget is somewhat like guardrails alongside a road. The guardrails must be placed relatively close to the edge of the road to keep vehicles from veering off their normal course; if the guardrails are placed in the middle of a field next to the road, they will be of no value.

ASSESSMENT

In addition to its use in planning and control, a budget is used to make ongoing assessments and rolling forecasts of financial results. It serves this function by providing a benchmark against which to compare results and signaling when course corrections are necessary. Results are assessed based on variances between budgeted amounts and actual results.

When things go according to plan, variances tend to remain positive throughout the year and approach zero as it draws to a close. When inflows and outflows are relatively uniform, variances tend to decline at a steady rate. Three months into a year, for instance, a variance might be around 75 percent of its original value; six months into the year, 50 percent; nine months into the year, 25 percent; and so on.

Signs of problems may exist on the revenue side if the variance percentage is higher than expected and on the expenditure side if it is lower than expected. For instance, if a business owner has budgeted $50,000 in sales revenue and $10,000 has been earned halfway through the year, the variance is $40,000, or 80 percent of its original value. That percentage is higher than 50 percent, so this may be a sign of problems depending on how steadily revenues are expected to be earned. If the owner has also budgeted $20,000 for supplies and has spent $15,000 halfway through the year, the variance is $5,000, or 25 percent of its original value. That percentage is too low if spending is expected to occur uniformly.

The opposite scenarios are not necessarily ideal, either. While revenue variances that are significantly lower than expected or expenditure variances that are significantly higher than expected may be a sign of outstanding performance, they can also be an indication of poor planning or inefficient use of resources. Assessments that are well off from expectations should be investigated to determine why, regardless of whether they are above or below their targets, in order to determine the cause and take corrective action if necessary.

The Importance of Budget Accuracy to Assessment

Just as budgeting accurately is important to planning and control functions, it is also important to assessment. An accurate budget tends to provide sound measures of performance and timely alerts when things are going off track. A budget that has been developed using an overly aggressive style tends to provide less reliable assessments. Take the example above, in which $50,000 of revenue was budgeted and $10,000 was earned halfway through the year. The assessment was that revenues were too low, since the variance was still 80 percent of its original value. This conclusion is valid only if it was reasonable to expect $50,000 of revenue in the first place. If annual revenues were typically around $20,000 in the past, the budget was probably too high from the start. To use an analogy, budgeting too aggressively is somewhat like making it a goal to master a craft in six months that normally takes many years to master.

Projections in overly cautious budgets do not serve as sound measures of performance, either. The difference is that using an overly aggressive style sets the bar too high and tends to generate false alarms, while using an overly cautious style sets it too low and can miss important warning signs. Say that in the preceding example the owner budgets $40,000 for supplies rather than $20,000. In this scenario, incurring $15,000 of expenses halfway through the year might be interpreted to mean that spending is being well managed. But if annual spending on supplies has never exceeded $20,000 in the past, there may be wasteful spending or other problems occurring that need to be investigated.

AN ADDITIONAL NOTE ON ASSESSMENT

Keep in mind that a full assessment of financial results should consider revenues and expenses together. If revenues are trending in the wrong direction but expenses are tracking in the right direction, for example, their effects will tend to offset one another. In addition, there may be variations in the rates at which revenues are earned and expenses are incurred throughout the year. These need to be taken into account when evaluating variance percentages and performance.

ACCOUNTING FOR RISK BY ADDING A CONTINGENCY ALLOWANCE

A budget represents a forecast of financial results, and the goal should be for that forecast to be as close as possible to the actual results. Despite our best efforts, though, the future is always at least somewhat uncertain. It may seem that the way to guard against this risk is to prepare for the worst-case scenario by budgeting very cautiously, but this causes inaccuracy that degrades a budget's usefulness for planning, control, and assessment.

A better approach is to develop the budget with a goal to be as accurate as possible—and then to add a reasonable contingency allowance as a final step. The contingency allowance should be budgeted in a separate account so that it does not distort areas of the budget that have been developed with precision in mind. As an example, an organization that has budgeted $10,000,000 for all anticipated expenses might add 3 percent to the total, budgeting $300,000 for unforeseeable events.

SUMMARY

A budget is used to manage financial position by serving as a tool to predict, control, and evaluate financial results. Accuracy is vital to a budget's utility for these purposes. Striving for accuracy in budgeting does not imply that risk cannot be accounted for. Reasonable contingency allowances can be budgeted in separate accounts to prepare for the unknown without sacrificing budget quality. Chapter 2 discusses statistical analysis methods and forecasting techniques that can be used for budgeting purposes.

Chapter 2

Statistical Measures and Methods

A certain amount of variance between budgetary estimates and actual results is to be expected, so the goal should be to minimize those variances by developing sound forecasts based on data and scientific methods. Using statistical analysis techniques to discern normal ranges and trends in historical data is a reasonable way to draw inferences about the future. Looking back five to ten years is often suitable.

HISTORICAL MEAN

One common approach to forecasting is to project future results based on the historical mean or average, which for the purposes of this discussion is calculated by dividing the total of all yearly values by the number of years in a data set:

Historical Mean = Total of All Yearly Values / Number of Years

An advantage of using the mean is that every data point is taken into consideration, while a disadvantage is that data points falling outside the normal range can distort the results. To illustrate the calculation of the mean, take a case in which the cost of electricity in each of the past five years was as follows:

  Year 1: $267,000
  Year 2: $270,000
  Year 3: $269,000
  Year 4: $272,000
  Year 5: $273,000

The total of all values is $1,351,000. Dividing that amount by five (the total number of years) yields an average of $270,200 per year.

HISTORICAL MEDIAN

An alternative approach to forecasting is to base projections on the historical median, which is the middle value in a data set placed in ascending order. Unlike the mean, the median is not skewed by outliers. However, it is not representative of all historical data. To determine the median in the data set just presented, first rearrange the values in numerical order:

$267,000; $269,000; $270,000; $272,000; $273,000

Next, determine the median by locating the value that has an equal number of data points to its left and to its right. In this case, that value is $270,000. Note that the median remains the same even if the values to its left are significantly reduced or if those to its right are significantly increased.

AVERAGE ANNUAL CHANGE

While the mean and median are sometimes appropriate for making forecasts, neither accounts for trends in the data. Notice in the data set analyzed above that there is a general upward trend, with the amount increasing from $267,000 in year 1 to $273,000 in year 5. Based on this, it is reasonable to predict that there will be another increase in year 6, but neither the mean nor the median is higher than the year 5 value. One way to account for data trends when making forecasts is to calculate the average annual change in values and then assume that this same change will occur in each future year. The average annual change can be calculated as:

Average Annual Change = (Final Value in Data Set − Beginning Value in Data Set) / (Number of Years of Data − 1)

The budget projection for the year following the final year can then be calculated:

Budget Projection = Final Value in Data Set + Average Annual Change

Using the values from the example, the calculation is:

Average Annual Change = ($273,000 − $267,000) / (5 − 1)
= $6,000 / 4
= $1,500
Budget Projection: $273,000 + $1,500 = $274,500

Note that the projection based on the average annual change is higher than those from the mean and median. This is because the upward trend in the data is considered when using the average annual change method. While this may be an improvement, a drawback is that only the beginning and ending values are taken into consideration to assess and measure the trend; that is, the projection would be the same regardless of the cost of electricity in years 2–4.

AVERAGE PERCENTAGE CHANGE

Another way to account for data trends is to base the forecast on the average percentage change in data set values. Using this method, all yearly percentage changes are calculated and averaged, and that average then serves as the basis for the budget projection. The percentage change from each year to the next is calculated using the following formula:

$$\text{Percentage Change from Year X to Year } (X + 1) = (\text{Year } [X + 1] \text{ Value} - \text{Year X Value}) / \text{Year X Value} \times 100$$

The budget projection then becomes:

$$\text{Budget Projection} = \text{Final Value in Data Set} \times (1 + \text{Average Percentage Change})$$

The procedure is as follows using the data from the example:

Percentage Change from Year 1 to Year 2: ($270,000 − $267,000) / $267,000 × 100 = 1.12%
Percentage Change from Year 2 to Year 3: ($269,000 − $270,000) / $270,000 × 100 = −0.37%
Percentage Change from Year 3 to Year 4: ($272,000 − $269,000) / $269,000 × 100 = 1.12%
Percentage Change from Year 4 to Year 5: ($273,000 − $272,000) / $272,000 × 100 = 0.37%
Average Percentage Change: (1.12% − 0.37% + 1.12% + 0.37%) / 4 = 0.56%
Budget Projection: $273,000 × (1 + 0.56%) = $274,529

LINEAR REGRESSION ANALYSIS

Linear regression analysis is a more advanced forecasting method that measures data trends by considering fluctuations across all data points and the timing of those fluctuations. This method derives a statistically defined best-fit line through the data points when they are plotted on a graph, and the line is then extended into the future to forecast future results. The math behind a linear regression analysis is rather complex, so using a software program to apply this method is recommended. To illustrate the basic steps using the previous data set, the first step is to plot the data points, as shown in figure 2.1.

Next, the best-fit line is added and the equation of the line displayed, as shown in figure 2.2.

In the equation, y represents the cost of electricity while x represents the year, so the equation can be rewritten as:

Cost of Electricity = $1,400 × Year + $266,000

Based on the linear regression analysis, the cost of electricity forecast in year 6 is $274,400:

$$\$1{,}400 \times 6 + \$266{,}000 = \$274{,}400$$

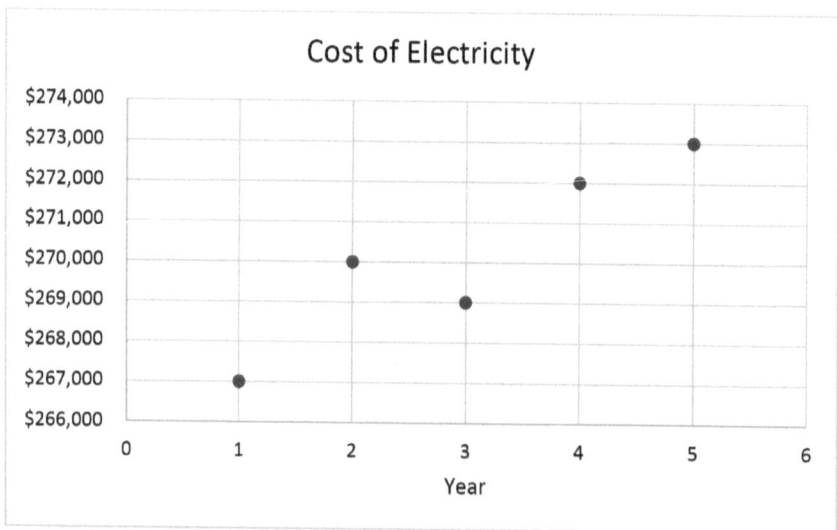

Figure 2.1. Plot of Electricity Costs

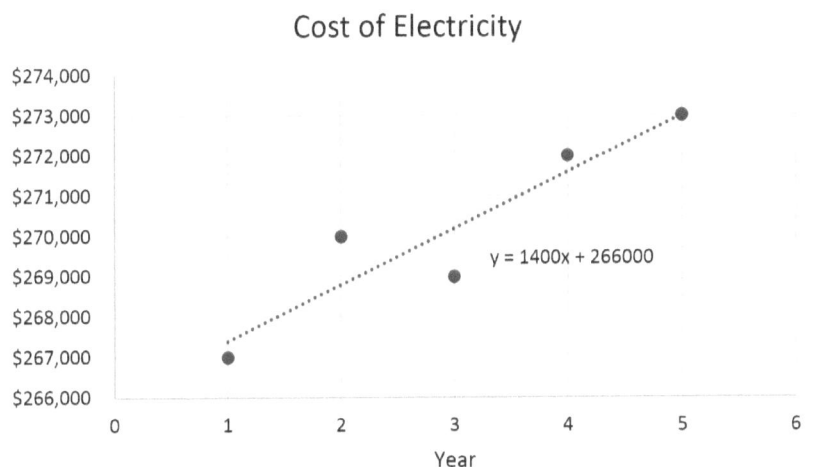

Figure 2.2. Linear Regression Analysis of Electricity Costs

The linear regression projects a slightly lower value than those based on the average annual change and average percentage change because it more effectively accounts for all yearly fluctuations and the timing of those fluctuations, particularly the decline in cost from year 2 to year 3.

MORE ADVANCED REGRESSION MODELS

While certainly an appropriate forecasting tool for some situations, linear regressions are somewhat simplistic because they assume a constant rate of change across all years. Other, more advanced regression models can be used when more nuanced analyses are desired. These models generate a best-fit curve through the data points rather than a best-fit line. By doing so, they often match historical patterns in the data more closely and provide more realistic forecasts. Examples of these techniques are exponential, logarithmic, and polynomial regressions. Figure 2.3 is a logarithmic regression analysis of the data from the example.

Substituting the cost of electricity for y and the year for x, the equation of the best-fit logarithmic curve can be rewritten as:

Cost of Electricity = $3,432.3 × \ln(\text{Year}) + $266,914

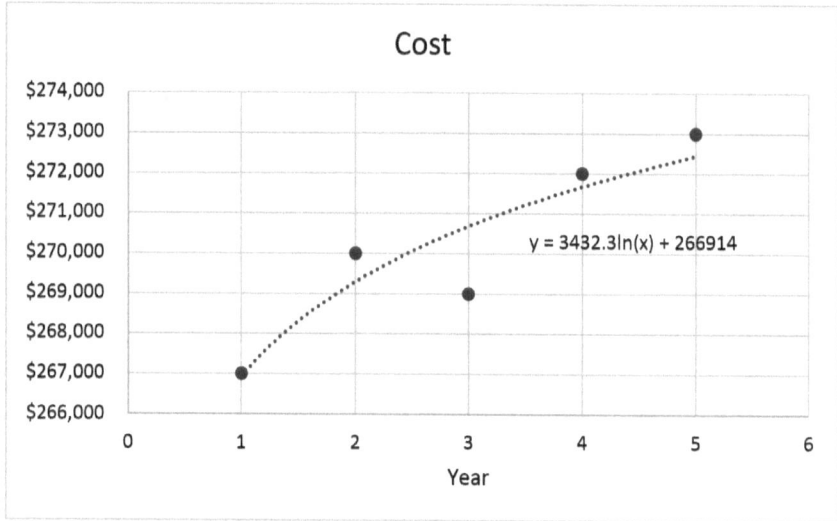

Figure 2.3. Logarithmic Regression Analysis of Electricity Costs

The logarithmic regression model forecast for the cost of electricity in year 6 is then $273,064:

$$\$3{,}432.3 \times \ln(6) + \$266{,}914 = \$273{,}064$$

Here the forecast is more moderate still, since the shape of the curve indicates a slowing growth rate over time.

Chapter 3

School District Operations and Expenses

Before learning about effective budgeting practices for school districts, it is helpful to be familiar with school district operations and the resources and costs they entail.

INSTRUCTIONAL SERVICES

Regular Instruction

The primary function of school districts is to educate students. To achieve this end, districts offer a number of instructional services, most of which are in the form of regular education courses. Examples of such courses are:

- History and Social Studies
- Language Arts
- Math
- Science
- Physical Education
- Art
- Music
- Business Education
- Computer Science
- Home Economics
- Industrial Arts

Special Education

In addition to providing regular instruction, districts are required to make accommodations for students with physical and learning disabilities under the

Individuals with Disabilities Education Act (IDEA) of 1997 and other laws that guarantee students with disabilities the right to participate in instructional programs to the greatest extent possible. Examples of special education services are:

- Early Intervention Programs
- Emotional Support
- Extended School Year Programs
- Gifted Support
- Hearing and Vision Support
- Life Skills and Learning Support
- Occupational and Physical Therapy
- Speech Language Support

The costs of these services can be highly variable and difficult to predict.

Special provisions are also required for students who are not proficient in English (English language learners; ELL) under Title VI of the Civil Rights Act of 1964. According to the US Department of Education Office for Civil Rights, this act was designed to ensure that these students can overcome language barriers and participate meaningfully in educational programs.[1]

INSTRUCTIONAL RESOURCES

Teachers and Aides

Resources are required to provide instructional services, and perhaps the first that come to mind are the teachers who work directly with students. Teachers with appropriate certifications work with special needs students, but some students need individualized attention that requires the assistance of instructional aides (also known as paraprofessionals). When teachers and aides are absent, school districts utilize substitutes, who may be direct employees or employees of a staffing agency.

Equipment and Supplies

Materials and equipment are also needed for instructional services, for example, furniture and desks for classrooms, computers and books for teaching, and smartboards used as interactive displays. In addition, assistive devices may be needed for some special education students: a student who struggles with taking notes might use an audio recorder to record lessons, or a student with vision challenges might use a large-screen or talking calculator.

Educational Software

Most school districts use educational software products to enhance instruction and facilitate learning. Teachers use software to develop curriculum, conduct online classes, and create and administer tests. Web-based assessment tools and grade books are used to evaluate and rate student performance. Students and teachers use messaging and collaboration apps to communicate with one another, and web-based games and interactive video lessons help to engage students in learning. Educational databases are used for research and learning, and online apps serve as learning aids to special education students.

Contracted Instructional Services

When school districts do not have the necessary resources to provide particular instructional services in-house, they often form agreements with outside contractors and professionals for the delivery of those services. A district that does not have a teacher qualified to work with ELL students may contract with a translation service, or a district without a speech therapist may use a speech-language pathologist who is an independent contractor.

District students sometimes directly enroll in outside institutions to receive educational services. For example, a hearing-impaired student may attend a school for deaf children, or a student with behavioral issues may attend an alternative education school. Students interested in pursuing a career in a trade may attend a vocational technical school, while those interested in theater may attend a performing arts charter school.

When outside institutions educate a district's students, they charge tuition. The amount charged is normally a function of the number of days of enrollment and the types of services provided. Tuition costs can be significant, particularly for special education students with high needs.

INSTRUCTIONAL SUPPORT

In addition to direct instructional services, school districts offer student support services. Nurses treat students suffering from illnesses or injuries, and guidance counselors provide academic and career advice. School psychologists provide psychological evaluations and therapy services for students suffering from emotional, mental health, and related issues, and librarians run school libraries, offering educational enrichment opportunities.

Like instructional programs, support activities require various supplies, technology products, and contracted services. School nurses use first aid kits to treat students and software to manage their health records, and guidance counselors use school counseling software to monitor student metrics and schedule appointments. School psychologists use record forms and response booklets for diagnostics and testing, and librarians manage online databases and catalogs for student use.

At times, outside professionals such as physicians and dentists also provide health-related services to students. The cost of these services might be based on a fixed fee or the number of examinations conducted, among other possible arrangements.

EDUCATIONAL ADMINISTRATION

Instructional and support services are delivered by teachers, paraprofessionals, support personnel, and outside professionals, but individuals are also needed to oversee these services. This is normally handled by a district's educational administration.

The number of educational administrators in a district often depends on its size. Smaller districts tend to have fewer administrators who wear many hats, while larger districts often have more administrators who each have a focused role. Educational administrators include curriculum directors, who manage academic programs and instructional materials; special education directors, who oversee services provided to special education students; principals, who oversee the operations within a particular school; and directors of student support services.

Educational administrators have many responsibilities and demands on their time. They typically have assistants who handle clerical tasks such as drafting correspondences, making copies, filing documents, and the like, allowing them to focus on leadership and management functions.

GRANTS ADMINISTRATION

School districts often receive grants from individuals, foundations, state and federal agencies, and other sources. Grants are awards that are to be used for a particular purpose, normally within a specified time period. Ways in which grant funds might be used include:

- Expanding and improving student mental health and emotional support services
- Hiring teachers to reduce class sizes or to expand special education services

- Implementing entrepreneurship classes, innovation spaces, or robotics labs
- Making safety and security enhancements to buildings
- Running prekindergarten programs
- Updating school curriculum

Districts must often submit financial and programmatic reports relating to the grants they receive to show that the funds were used as intended and the desired programmatic outcomes were achieved. Effective grants administration requires careful planning, close monitoring of spending, and strong record-keeping systems that can easily produce backup documentation for submitted reports when requested. Due to the complexity of grants administration, districts commonly employ grant managers to handle some or all of these functions. These individuals are often part of the administrative team.

When budgeting for grants, total projected expenditures should match the grant award. For instance, the following expenditures might be budgeted under a $50,000 technology grant:

Computers: $25,000
Printers: $10,000
Network cabling upgrades: $15,000
Total: $50,000

The time period within which a grant must be spent, or the grant term, typically ranges from one to five years. For those grants that span multiple years, total costs in all years combined must equal the total award. For example, expenses under a $1 million grant that covers three years might be $500,000 in year 1, $300,000 in year 2, and $200,000 in year 3.

ANCILLARY STUDENT SERVICES

Extracurricular Activities

In addition to their core instructional services, school districts also provide students with opportunities to take part in various extracurricular activities. Athletic programs allow students to participate in various sports, and student councils provide a chance to learn about leadership and governance. Art and foreign language clubs provide creative outlets and exposure to other cultures, and drama clubs provide outlets for those interested in the performing arts. Band and chorus programs are other examples of offerings outside the normal course of study.

Student Transportation

Another ancillary service provided by school districts is student transportation. Districts may have their own drivers, buses, vans, and other vehicles, or they may contract with a transportation provider such as a bus company. When transportation is handled internally, personnel, vehicle maintenance, fuel, and other related costs are incurred. When it is contracted out, transportation providers charge for their services, often basing their fees on factors such as the types of vehicles provided, the number and length of runs, and special accommodations that are required. As an example, transportation for a special education student who requires a specialized van and personal aide and is transported over long distances would tend to be quite expensive.

Most transportation occurs at the beginning and end of the school day, when students travel to and from school, but may also be required when students participate in field trips, athletic competitions, and other events. Some districts with high population density, where all students live within walking distance of school, may provide transportation only for outside events or special education students who have a documented need for this service.

Food Service

School districts also operate food service programs that serve meals, a la carte items, vending machine products, and more. These programs may also provide catering services for special events. Food service operations are normally budgeted separately from other school district operations.

PLANT OPERATIONS

Plant operations involve the maintenance of physical assets such as buildings and equipment as well as exterior grounds. This maintenance is done to ensure safety and maximize efficiency as well as for aesthetic reasons.

Buildings

School districts vary in size in terms of geographical area and student enrollment. Some very small districts may have just one school housing all grades, while others consist of more than one school. Often each school is designated for certain grade levels. One possible configuration is a district consisting of a primary school for students in kindergarten through grade 2, an elementary school for those in grades 3 through 5, a middle school for those in grades 6 through 8, and a high school for those in grades 9 through 12. Larger districts often have multiple schools of the same type (e.g., four elementary schools), each designated for students living in a certain area of the district.

Individual schools may serve other purposes as well. For example, a very large district might have schools that serve special education students only or science and technology academies for students who are interested in pursuing a career in those areas. Districts often have other buildings, too, such as administrative centers and garages.

School buildings consist of an intricate network of systems and components. HVAC systems consist of boilers, heating units, chillers, and other equipment, while plumbing systems are made up of pipes, fixtures, drains, and so forth. Electrical systems consist of components such as generators, transformers, panels, and circuits, and fire and safety systems are made up of alarms, sprinklers, access control devices, and other devices.

In addition to maintenance and upkeep, building costs include utilities such as electricity, water and sewage, and natural gas, as well as phone lines and networks.

Construction Costs

When a school building is constructed, many parties are involved, and the costs are significant. In addition to school district personnel, there are architects and engineers who design the building layout and systems, general contractors and subcontractors who perform the labor, and construction managers who supervise the work and make sure it is done in accordance with design specifications. In addition to the cost of these services, there are many other expenses, such as those for materials, surveys, and site upgrades, as well as building inspections and permits.

Because construction projects are very expensive, they are normally financed through loans, often in the form of bond issuances. This process entails additional costs for financial advisers, underwriters, ratings agencies, and attorneys, among others.

Equipment and Grounds

Other equipment must be maintained as well, such as:

- Forklifts and other lifting devices
- Lawnmowers and tractors
- Vacuum cleaners and carpet scrubbers
- Machinery and appliances

Lawns, trees, and shrubbery; athletic fields and playgrounds; and driveways, parking lots, and sidewalks also require regular maintenance.

When district employees handle custodial and maintenance functions internally, they need supplies and tools to do their jobs. Soap, detergents, and other products are used for cleaning, and tools such as screwdrivers, wrenches, and hammers are needed for repairs. Paint is used to spruce up rooms, and topsoil and fertilizer are used for landscaping.

Plant Contracted Services

When in-house employees do not have the requisite knowledge or background to complete certain maintenance tasks or repairs, districts often pay outsiders—such as electricians, plumbers, and mechanical contractors—to do the work. Even when there is the capacity to do the work in house, it is sometimes more cost effective to pay an outside organization, as may be the case when hiring a painting company to paint a gymnasium or a landscaping company to handle lawn care. Some districts go so far as to outsource all their custodial and maintenance functions to a facilities management service.

When outside contractors are used for ongoing maintenance and repairs, a possible billing arrangement is one in which a set periodic fee is charged for recurring maintenance and additional fees are charged for repairs falling outside the standard routine.

Inspections and Tests

Along with general maintenance and repairs, some types of equipment are inspected and tested on a regular cycle to ensure continuing safety. This may include:

- Elevators and chairlifts
- Fire extinguishers, alarms, and sprinkler systems
- Backflow prevention devices
- Backstops for basketball courts
- Stage rigging systems
- Buses, vans, and trucks

Periodic tests might also be done to inspect for asbestos or to measure lead and copper levels in drinking water.

Replacements and Renovations

Strong maintenance programs help to prolong the useful lives of assets, but even the best programs cannot forestall the need for replacements and renovations indefinitely. At some point, a leaky roof that has been patched many times will need to be replaced, or a vehicle that has been repaired many times will no longer be salvageable. Likewise, a parking lot that has been recoated and patched over a period of several years will eventually need to be replaced with new asphalt.

While some replacements and renovations are required, others are more a matter of choice. For example, building windows that are still functional may be replaced to provide better insulation, new high-efficiency lighting may be installed to reduce utility bills, or a new HVAC control system may be installed to improve climate control and reduce energy consumption.

Oversight

Like other school district operations, plant operations require oversight. Those who handle this function may be referred to as building and grounds directors, facilities managers, or some other title. Common responsibilities of this position are:

- Scheduling, coordinating, and supervising cleaning, maintenance, and repair work
- Ensuring that ample cleaning supplies, equipment, and tools are on hand
- Scheduling and documenting inspections
- Reviewing and monitoring maintenance contracts
- Recommending and planning capital projects and renovations

SECURITY

To maintain a secure environment, school buildings commonly have intrusion detection and door access control systems. These systems often include access control software, electric locks, fob readers, motion sensors, and keypads, among other components. In addition, security guards, police officers, or school resource officers are often used to maintain order and build relationships with students in order to promote a positive climate. These individuals may be directly employed, independent contractors, or employees of a police department or security guard service.

TECHNOLOGY OPERATIONS

As previously discussed, technology is utilized in various ways by teachers and students. Technology also has applications well beyond the classroom that extend to virtually all school district operations. A technology network consists of many components; just a few examples include:

- Servers and switches
- Firewalls and content filters
- Computers and handheld devices
- Enterprise resource planning software
- Smartboards and projectors
- Instructional software products
- Student information systems
- Copiers, printers, and scanners
- Fax machines and phone systems
- Work order management software

Technology networks are complex and require skilled management. This function can be handled by an in-house manager and team or an outside technology management company.

BUSINESS OPERATIONS

Effective financial management is essential to ensuring the ongoing viability of school districts. This function is normally handled by a business administrator (also referred to as business manager, finance director, or chief financial officer, among other titles) who oversees processes and procedures such as:

- Financial planning and budgeting
- Financial reporting and analysis
- Purchasing and receiving
- Payment processing
- Invoicing
- Cash-handling procedures
- Payroll processing
- Employee benefits program management
- Account management and reconciliations

Business administrators are also in charge of risk management procedures, implementing internal controls over processes where there is a high risk of error or fraud, such as those involving the handling of cash and other assets. Business administrators also purchase insurance policies that help to mitigate risk by covering expenses from property damage, lawsuits, data breaches, ransomware attacks, and other incidents that could create a loss. Umbrella policies are often purchased to provide coverage that activates when the limits of the other policies are reached.

As public entities, school districts are required to undergo recurring audits. Business administrators oversee this process by making sure the auditors have all financial and other information they need and responding to their questions. Audit firms typically base their billing on factors such as the number and types of programs to be examined, the amount of time spent on the audit, and the complexity of the engagement.

BOARD AND CENTRAL OPERATIONS

School boards consist of local representatives who are responsible for establishing district goals and policies. The board's role is to provide governance and to oversee a team of administrators it hires to develop, implement, and manage processes to achieve the stated goals.

The superintendent is the chief executive officer whose job is to lead, set the overall tone of the organization, and run the district's central office. This individual acts as a liaison between the board and administration, assisting and advising the board as it crafts its goals and policies and leading the administrative team's efforts to achieve those goals.

There are numerous and complex laws and regulations that school districts are required to adhere to. Some of these are designed to protect the rights of students, such as IDEA. Others are designed to protect the rights of employees, such as the Civil Rights Act of 1964, which makes workplace discrimination illegal. There are many other laws pertaining to school district operations that school boards and superintendents must be cognizant of. Having appropriate legal counsel to guide them through legal issues that arise is crucial. Attorney fee structures typically include a monthly retainer for ongoing availability and additional hourly charges for services not covered by the retainer agreement.

PUBLIC RELATIONS

The school board represents the surrounding community and works with the superintendent to ensure that the district's goals and policies represent the public interest. Despite this, at times it may be necessary for the administration to communicate directly with the public. For example, parents may need to be notified of a threat to the health and safety of students or a school closure due to weather conditions. There may also be positive news to share, such as the implementation of new and innovative educational programs or the accomplishments of students. In an effort to communicate effectively and maintain a positive image, districts may have a public relations expert on staff or contract with a public relations firm that assists them with crafting messages.

PERSONNEL COSTS

School districts require resources to operate, the most expensive of which are usually their employees. Employee compensation and benefits, particularly for teachers, typically make up a large percentage of a school district's overall expenses.

Employee Compensation

Teachers, administrators, and managers are typically paid an annual salary, while other employees such as instructional aides, office assistants, custodians, and maintenance personnel are more likely to be paid an hourly wage. Most hourly employees are covered by the Fair Labor Standards Act, which, according to the US Department of Labor, stipulates that they "must receive overtime pay for hours worked in excess of 40 hours in a workweek of at least one and one-half times their regular rates of pay."[2] Some earnings can be in the form of stipends or bonuses as well.

Employee Benefits

FICA (Social Security and Medicare)

In addition to salaries and wages, employees receive benefits, some of which are legally mandated. One example is employer FICA contributions, which are used to fund a portion of Social Security and Medicare benefits for employees. In 2022, the employer Social Security rate was 6.2 percent of each employee's earnings up to $147,000, while the Medicare rate was

1.45 percent of all earnings, making the FICA rate 7.65 percent for most employees.

Pensions

Pensions are another employee benefit. Most states provide defined benefit pension plans to public school employees, and several offer defined contribution plans as alternatives. Pension funds are partly made up of school district contributions.

Health Insurance

Yet another employee benefit is health insurance. Health insurance premiums are influenced by a variety of factors, such as location, the number of individuals covered, and the number and types of medical services covered. Premiums are also affected by plan deductibles and copays. A common arrangement is for school districts to pay the full premium for each employee and then to withhold a portion of their pay to offset some of the cost.

Workers' Compensation and Unemployment Compensation

School districts also pay for workers' compensation and unemployment compensation insurance coverage for employees. Workers' compensation insurance is provided to cover costs resulting from workplace illnesses and injuries. Factors such as a district's size and location and the frequency and severity of past reported claims influence the premiums for this type of insurance. Price trends within the general insurance market also affect premiums.

Unemployment tax is paid at both the federal and state levels. The net Federal Unemployment Tax Act (FUTA) tax is 0.6 percent of the first $7,000 paid to each employee subject to FUTA tax in most states.[3] State unemployment tax rates vary.

PROFESSIONAL DEVELOPMENT AND TRAVEL

In order to stay up to date on the latest industry trends and best practices, school districts often pay for employee memberships in professional organizations. When employees sign up for and participate in classes, seminars, and training programs offered by these organizations, additional registration fees and travel costs for mileage, meals, and lodging may be incurred.

SUPPLIES AND EQUIPMENT

The cost of supplies and equipment needed for operations consists of the purchase price and shipping and installation charges. Additional charges for taxes, licenses, subscriptions, and warranties may also apply in some cases.

As public entities, school districts must adhere to certain standards when purchasing goods. This helps to ensure responsible stewardship of tax funds. Existing federal regulations require districts to solicit at least three price quotes when using federal funds for the purchase of equipment or supplies exceeding $10,000 in cost. In addition to federal requirements, districts must follow applicable state laws and regulations governing procurement.

Sometimes equipment is leased rather than owned. Copiers, computers, fax machines, and telephones are a few examples of equipment that might be leased.

NOTES

1. US Department of Education Office for Civil Rights, "Developing Programs for English Language Learners: Legal Background," last modified January 16, 2020, https://www2.ed.gov/about/offices/list/ocr/ell/legal.html.

2. US Department of Labor, "Overtime Pay," https://www.dol.gov/general/topic/wages/overtimepay.

3. Jeff Oswald, "What Does an Unemployment Claim Cost an Employer?" Unemployment Insurance Services, https://unemployment-services.com/unemployment-claim-cost-employer/#:~:text=Unemployment%20is%20funded%2C%20and%20taxed,%E2%80%9D%20reducing%20that%20to%200.6%25.

Chapter 4

Budgeting School District Expenses

As school districts incur expenses, their available financial resources decline. Having adequate resources on hand at all times is critical, so developing an expenditure budget—a financial plan that forecasts expenses in the upcoming fiscal year—is also essential.

PERSONNEL EXPENSES

Personnel expenses for employee compensation and benefits typically make up the largest expenditure category in a school district budget, and teachers almost always make up the most expensive employee group.

EMPLOYEE COMPENSATION

Employee compensation consists of salaries, wages, stipends, and other forms of payment.

Teacher Salaries

Teachers frequently belong to unions that negotiate their compensation in collective bargaining agreements (CBAs). These agreements often contain salary schedules that establish compensation levels based on criteria such as the year of the agreement and the level of experience and educational credentials of teachers. Table 4.1 is a section of a hypothetical teacher salary schedule.

Salary schedules are used during the budgeting process to determine each teacher's salary in the upcoming year by identifying their position in the schedule in the current year and then shifting them to the appropriate position

Yrs. Experience	Year 1		Year 2	
	Bachelor's	Master's	Bachelor's	Master's
0	$50,000	$52,000	$51,000	$53,100
1	$53,000	$55,200	$54,000	$56,300
2	$56,100	$58,500	$57,100	$59,600
3	$59,300	$61,900	$60,300	$63,000

Table 4.1. Teacher Salary Schedule

for the subsequent year. Referring to table 4.1, if during year 1 a teacher with a master's degree has two years of experience, their salary is $58,500. Their year 2 salary is then determined by moving down one row to add a year of experience and to the right two columns to move to the next year. This reveals that the teacher's year 2 salary will be $63,000.

To illustrate using a more advanced scenario, assume that in total there are eighteen teachers with two years or less of experience distributed throughout the schedule as follows in year 1:

- Four with a bachelor's degree and no years of experience (Group A)
- Three with a master's degree and one year of experience (Group B)
- Five with a bachelor's degree and two years of experience (Group C)
- Six with a master's degree and two years of experience (Group D)

To budget the year 2 salaries during year 1, first determine whether the employment status or educational credentials of any teachers are expected to change from one year to the next. For the purposes of this example, say that the only anticipated changes by the start of year 2 are that two teachers in Group A are expected to have their master's degrees and that one teacher in Group D is expected to be employed elsewhere based on a notice they have submitted.

Making these adjustments and adding one year of experience for each teacher who will remain, the year 2 distribution is:

- Two with a bachelor's degree and one year of experience (Group A1)
- Two with a master's degree and one year of experience (Group A2)
- Three with a master's degree and two years of experience (Group B)
- Five with a bachelor's degree and three years of experience (Group C)
- Five with a master's degree and three years of experience (Group D)

Note that Group A has been split into two to account for the anticipated changes in educational credentials and that Group D consists of one fewer teacher to reflect the anticipated resignation.

Next, determine each group's per-teacher salary in year 2 based on the salary schedule:

Group A1: $54,000
Group A2: $56,300
Group B: $59,600
Group C: $60,300
Group D: $63,000

The total year 2 salaries of each group can then be calculated by multiplying the number of teachers by the per-teacher salary:

Group A1: 2 teachers × $54,000 per teacher = $108,000
Group A2: 2 teachers × $56,300 per teacher = $112,600
Group B: 3 teachers × $59,600 per teacher = $178,800
Group C: 5 teachers × $60,300 per teacher = $301,500
Group D: 5 teachers × 63,000 per teacher = $315,000

Adding the total salaries for each group reveals that the total of the salaries that should be budgeted for year 2 for all groups combined is $1,015,900.

Other Employee Salaries

Budgeting the salaries of other employees like administrators and managers is usually just a matter of adding appropriate percentages to their current salaries based on the terms of employment contracts or agreements.

Regular Wages

Employees who are not managers or teachers are typically paid an hourly wage. The following formula can be used to budget the regular wages of an hourly employee:

Regular Wages = Regular Hourly Wage × Hours Worked per Year

To illustrate, the budget for the regular wages of a custodian who makes $18.50 per hour and works eight hours per day, 260 days per year is calculated as follows:

Regular Wages = $18.50 per Hour × Hours Worked per Year
Hours Worked per Year = 8 Hours per Day × 260 Days per Year = 2,080
Regular Wages = $18.50 per Hour × 2,080 Hours per Year
= $38,480

Overtime

Wage employees must be paid at an overtime rate of at least one and one half times their regular rate of pay for work in excess of forty hours in a week. The formulas to budget overtime are:

$$\text{Overtime Rate} = \text{Regular Hourly Wage} \times 1.5$$
$$\text{Overtime} = \text{Overtime Rate} \times \text{Estimated Annual Overtime Hours}$$

If it is estimated that the custodian discussed above will work ten hours of overtime throughout the course of the year in addition to their regular hours, the amount that should be budgeted for their overtime is calculated as follows:

$$\text{Overtime} = \text{Overtime Rate} \times 10 \text{ Estimated Overtime Hours}$$
$$\text{Overtime Rate} = \$18.50 \text{ per Hour} \times 1.5 = \$27.75 \text{ per Hour}$$
$$\text{Overtime} = \$27.75 \text{ per Hour} \times 10 \text{ Estimated Overtime Hours}$$
$$= \$277.50$$

Substitute Pay

When teachers are absent, substitutes who work as direct employees are normally paid an hourly or daily rate. Because future absenteeism rates are uncertain, the budget for substitutes must be estimated in most cases.

EMPLOYEE BENEFITS

FICA (Social Security and Medicare)

In addition to salaries and wages, personnel costs include employee benefits. One example of these is employer FICA contributions, which consist of Social Security and Medicare contributions made on behalf of employees. Because these are a percentage of employee earnings, budgeting the cost of FICA is straightforward once the earnings are budgeted. The formulas to budget employer FICA contributions for each employee are:

$$\text{FICA Contributions} = \text{Social Security Contributions}$$
$$+ \text{Medicare Contributions}$$
$$\text{Social Security Contributions} = \text{Employee Earnings up to } \$147,000 \times 6.2\%$$
$$\text{Medicare Contributions} = \text{Employee Earnings} \times 1.45\%$$

For employees earning $147,000 or less, the formula simplifies to:

FICA Contributions = Employee Earnings × 7.65%

Suppose that a district central office consists of a superintendent and office assistant. In the upcoming year, the superintendent will earn $200,000 and the office assistant will earn $50,000. To budget the cost of Social Security for each, first determine the amount of their earnings that will be subject to Social Security. The superintendent's earnings are above the $147,000 threshold, so only that amount will be subject to Social Security tax. On the other hand, all of the office assistant's earnings will be taxed, since they are below the threshold. Applying this information, the amount of Social Security to budget for each is:

Social Security Contributions (Superintendent) = $147,000 × 6.2% = $9,114
Social Security Contributions (Office Assistant) = $50,000 × 6.2% = $3,100

Budgeting the cost of Medicare is slightly easier, since all earnings are subject to Medicare tax. The amounts to budget for this tax are:

Medicare Contributions (Superintendent) = $200,000 × 1.45% = $2,900
Medicare Contributions (Office Assistant) = $50,000 × 1.45% = $725

The budgeted cost of employer FICA contributions made on behalf of both employees is then:

$9,114 + $3,100 + $2,900 + $725 = $15,839

Pensions

Pension contributions made on behalf of employees are budgeted by multiplying employee earnings by the employer contribution rate in a district's state.

Health Insurance

School districts provide various types of insurance coverage to employees, the most expensive of which is ordinarily health insurance. The employee contribution toward their premiums for this insurance is generally withheld from their pay. For example, if in the upcoming year a district will pay $1,700 per month for family coverage for a twelve-month employee and will withhold $200 per month from their pay for the cost of this insurance, the budget for the net cost of the employee's health insurance is calculated as follows:

$$\text{Annual Premium} = \$1{,}700 \text{ per month} \times 12 \text{ months} = \$20{,}400$$
$$\text{Employee Contributions} = \$200 \text{ per month} \times 12 \text{ months} = \$2{,}400$$
$$\text{Net Annual Premium} = \$18{,}000$$

Workers' Compensation Insurance

Workers' compensation insurance is budgeted by apportioning its cost to each employee based on their earnings. For instance, the amount assigned to each employee might be 0.5 percent of their earnings. This percentage is manipulated until the total assigned to all employees matches the estimated or quoted cost of the insurance policy.

Unemployment Compensation Insurance (Federal)

Because the FUTA tax is 0.6 percent of the first $7,000 paid to each employee in most cases, the formula to budget the cost of this tax in these cases is:

$$\text{FUTA Tax} = \text{Number of Employees Making at Least } \$7{,}000 \times \$42 + \text{Total Earnings of Employees Making Less Than } \$7{,}000 \times 0.6\%$$

For instance, if a group of ten employees consists of eight full-time employees who will make more than $7,000, one seasonal employee who will make $6,000, and one part-time employee who will make $5,000, the calculation is:

$$\text{FUTA Tax} = 8 \times \$42 + (\$6{,}000 + \$5{,}000) \times 0.6\%$$
$$8 \times \$42 + \$11{,}000 \times 0.6\% = \$402$$

NON-PERSONNEL COSTS

Loan and Lease Payments

When debt is issued, a repayment schedule establishes when future payments of principal and interest will be due. Budgeting these payments is simply a matter of totaling the amounts in the schedule for the upcoming year.

Equipment leases can often be budgeted rather easily as well. For example, if a district is leasing copiers for $7,000 per month and the agreement extends into the following year, then $84,000 should be budgeted.

Contracted Services

Service agreements with outside providers often require payments on a set schedule. When this is the case, the amount to budget for these payments can be readily determined. Examples might include:

- Monthly tuition payments for a student attending an outside educational institution
- Monthly payments under a legal retainer agreement
- Quarterly payments under a preventive maintenance agreement for mechanical equipment
- Quarterly payments for a wide area network service

On the other hand, some contracted service costs may have to be approximated, such as diagnostic fees and travel and labor charges for work falling outside a scope of services covered by an agreement.

Supplies and Equipment

When specific supplies and equipment have been identified for purchase in the upcoming year and their prices are known, they can be budgeted precisely. An example would be books that will be purchased from a particular vendor that has listed the prices of the books on its website. On the other hand, the cost of consumable supplies such as paper, pens, folders, and ink cartridges may have to be estimated if they are purchased on an as-needed basis.

Membership Dues

Budgeting professional association membership dues is normally just a matter of finding out what the rates will be for the upcoming year and multiplying those rates by the number of memberships needed.

Insurance

The cost of insurance policies to protect a school district from financial loss due to property damage, lawsuits, cyberattacks, and other unfortunate events can be budgeted exactly once quotes for coverage from insurers have been received and accepted. Prior to that, they can be included as estimates in earlier versions of the budget.

OTHER NON-PERSONNEL COSTS

The following non-personnel costs must be estimated for budgeting purposes:

- Tuition for unknown future students who will be enrolled in outside educational institutions
- Equipment repairs
- Utilities
- Capital project change orders
- Tax refunds
- Fees for legal services outside a standard retainer agreement

Chapter 5

Budgeting School District Revenues

As public entities, school districts receive funds from a combination of local, state, and federal sources. Local and state sources provide about 90 percent of these funds; federal sources make up the rest. Just as budgeting expenses is an essential part of financial planning, so too is budgeting revenues.

LOCAL FUNDING

Local Taxes

Local revenue is generated primarily by taxes, most of which are in the form of property taxes. In 2018–2019, 80 percent of school district taxes in the United States were in the form of property taxes.[1] The school tax on a property is the product of its assessment and the property tax rate:

Property Tax Charged = Property Assessment × Property Tax Rate

Depending on where a district is located, assessment information may be provided by state, county, or city governments, among other possible information sources. The property tax rate may be expressed in mills, with one mill being equal to 0.001. When this convention is used, the preceding formula can be rewritten as:

Property Tax Charged = Property Assessment
× Property Tax Rate (mills) × 0.001

As an example, the tax charged on a property assessed at $250,000 in a school district with a property tax rate of 20 mills would be:

$250,000 \times 20 \times 0.001 = \$5,000$

The total property tax a school district charges in a given year for all properties combined is the total assessment of all properties (tax base) multiplied by the property tax rate:

Total Property Tax Charged on All Properties = Total Assessment of All Properties × Property Tax Rate (mills) × 0.001

If a school district with a property tax rate of 17 mills consists of ten thousand properties with an average assessment of $150,000, the total property tax charged is calculated as follows:

Total Property Tax Charged on All Properties = Total Assessment of All Properties × 17 × 0.001
Total Assessment of All Properties = 10,000 × $150,000 = $1,500,000,000
$1,500,000,000 × 17 × 0.001 = $25,500,000

For various reasons, a certain percentage of taxes charged is not collected each year. The total that is actually collected represents property tax revenue and is represented by the following formula:

Property Tax Revenue = Total Property Tax Charged on All Properties × Collection Percentage

If the collection percentage in our example district is 95 percent, its property tax revenue can be calculated as follows:

$25,500,000 × 0.95 = \$24,225,000$

When budgeting property tax revenue, estimates must be made as to what the collection percentage will be. Historical collection rates can provide insight into what that percentage might be in a given year. The collection percentage is the ratio of the taxes collected in that year to the taxes charged:

Collection Percentage = Total Taxes Collected / Total Taxes Charged on All Properties

It is also necessary to estimate the total assessment of all properties when property taxes charged in the upcoming fiscal year will be based on assessments on a future billing date. This is because assessments may fluctuate in the interim. When estimating assessments, it is important to be aware of factors that could significantly impact property values, such as major assessment appeals that are pending or new commercial developments that are underway.

School districts may also impose other taxes, such as income or sales tax, depending on the state in which they are located. These taxes can be budgeted using a procedure similar to that used to budget property tax revenue. The difference is that when calculating total income or sales tax charged, total income or sales replaces the total assessment of all properties as the tax base, and the income or sales tax rate replaces the property tax rate. An alternative approach is simply to base the budget amounts on the total revenue generated by each tax in prior years.

Investment Income

While taxes are the primary source of local revenue for school districts, there are other sources of income as well. Investment income is one example. When funds are invested in an account that offers a fixed rate of return and no further deposits or withdrawals occur, annual interest income can be budgeted using the following formula:

$$\text{Interest Income} = \text{Amount Invested at Beginning of Year} \times \text{Effective Interest Rate}$$

As an example, $1 million invested in an account offering an effective rate of 3 percent will generate $30,000 in interest:

$$\$1,000,000 \times 0.03 = \$30,000$$

On the other hand, income from investments in variable-rate accounts such as a savings or money market account must be estimated.

Local Grants

Local revenues can also come from grants that have been awarded. A local grant might be in the form of an award from a nearby technology company to implement a computer lab or funding from a local foundation for district administrators to attend a national conference. There are many possible uses of local grant funds.

In some cases, revenues from local grants can be budgeted precisely. For instance, if a school district has been informed by a foundation that it will be providing a grant of $5,000 to be used to pay for staff professional development in the upcoming fiscal year, the amount of revenue to budget from the grant is known. Some grants that will be received are not known ahead of time, though. Future revenues from these grants must be estimated.

Other Local Revenue

Examples of other local revenues include:

- Admission fees to school events
- Proceeds from renting out school facilities
- Website advertising fees
- Donations

Most commonly budgeted revenues from these sources are approximations based on analyses of historical data and other information that may be pertinent.

STATE FUNDING

State Subsidies

States often distribute subsidies to school districts to help offset costs that are incurred as a result of:

- Regular education programs
- Special education programs
- Student transportation services
- Student health services
- Tuition charges
- FICA and pension contributions
- Debt service payments

State subsidies are typically divided among school districts using formulas that apportion funds based on criteria such as:

- Geographical size and student enrollment
- Population density
- Number of English language learner students
- Property values
- Resident income levels

Generally speaking, these formulas are designed to increase the amount of state aid to districts that are larger, are more densely populated, have more students with intense needs, and are less affluent.

Ideally, funding formulas can be used during the budgeting process to determine the amounts a school district will receive from state subsidies in the subsequent year. Things are not always this straightforward, though. Funding formulas are often very complex and may require a number of data inputs that are not readily available. Moreover, the formulas themselves may not yet be finalized by state legislatures at the time school districts are preparing their budgets. Professional school business associations can be invaluable resources by assisting in deciphering the formulas, estimating data inputs and award amounts, and monitoring legislative developments.

State Grants

State funding can also be distributed in the form of grants. Targeted grants may be provided for things like instructional equipment, technology improvements, security upgrades, and programs such as pre-K and Head Start. These are often competitive grants that require the submission of applications detailing how the funds will be spent and outcomes achieved. Grant applications in process should be reviewed while the budget is being developed in order to project the amount of revenue they might generate.

FEDERAL FUNDING

Title Grants

A large amount of federal money is distributed to school districts through title grants under the Elementary and Secondary Education Act of 1965. For instance, Title I, Part A grants provide financial assistance to educate children from low-income families, and Title II, Part A grants are used by districts to improve the quality of teaching and instruction. Title III grants help to pay for the instruction of ELL and immigrant students, and Title IV, Part B grants provide funding for the implementation of after-school programs in low-performing schools. Several other title grants exist as well.[2]

In order to qualify to receive title grants, school districts must complete a rigorous application process, submitting written narratives and budgets detailing how the funds will be used. Districts must also submit signed certifications attesting that they will spend the funds in a manner that ensures fair competition and abides by all federal procurement laws, that they will comply with all reporting requirements, and that they have policies in place to prevent conflicts of interest.

Budgeting revenues from title grants requires a review of federal awards that are pending or already approved. If there are district grant managers who oversee federal awards, they should be included in this review.

IDEA Funds

In addition to title funds, some federal money is distributed under the Individuals with Disabilities Education Act of 1997. This law was enacted to ensure that special education students receive appropriate educational services, so IDEA grant revenues are used to implement programs and pay for resources to accomplish this end. District special education directors often oversee the use of IDEA funds and can assist in budgeting IDEA revenues.

Other Federal Assistance

The federal government may provide funds to school districts to assist them in running preschool, vocational education, and adult education programs. Federal funds are also used to educate children experiencing homelessness and serve nutritious meals to students.

Emergency Federal Assistance

The federal government frequently intervenes when calamities occur by providing financial and other assistance to school districts. For example, in the aftermath of Hurricane Katrina in 2005, the Federal Emergency Management Agency stepped in to provide emergency support that was used to restore thousands of school buildings and facilities in Louisiana. When the 2008 financial crisis hit, the American Recovery and Reinvestment Act was passed to provide stimulus funding to school districts, helping them preserve jobs. Following the COVID-19 outbreak in early 2020, various federal laws were passed to distribute money to schools from the Elementary and Secondary School Emergency Relief Fund. These included the Coronavirus Aid, Relief, and Economic Security Act of 2020; Coronavirus Response and Relief Supplemental Appropriations Act of 2021; and American Rescue Plan Act of 2021.

Federal emergency assistance payments are sometimes made over several years to coincide with the amount of time a full recovery is expected to take. When emergency funds that have been awarded will be distributed in the upcoming year, they should be included as part of the overall revenue budget.

NOTES

1. National Center for Education Statistics, "Public School Revenue Sources," last updated May 2022, https://nces.ed.gov/programs/coe/indicator/cma.
2. Department of Education Office of Elementary and Secondary Education, "Improving Basic Programs Operated by Local Educational Agencies (ESEA Title I, Part A)," last updated November 5, 2020, https://oese.ed.gov/offices/office-of-formula-grants/school-support-and-accountability/title-i-part-a-program/; Pennsylvania Office of the Budget, "Chart of Accounts for PA Local Educational Agencies, 2021–2022 FY," https://www.education.pa.gov/Teachers%20-%20Administrators/School%20Finances/Office%20of%20Comptroller%20Operations/Accounting/Pages/default.aspx, last updated October 25, 2021; National Association of Secondary School Principals, "Title IV—21st Century Schools," https://www.nassp.org/a/title-iv-21st-century-schools.

Chapter 6

The Budget Layout

A school district budget consists of two parts: an expenditure budget and a revenue budget. Each of these contains multiple accounts, and it is important to organize them in a logical manner.

EXPENDITURE BUDGET LAYOUT

The expenditure budget can be organized in various ways. One common approach is to group accounts by functional area. The following is a list of common functional areas:

- Regular Education
- Special Education
- Instructional Support Services
- Ancillary Student Services
- Educational Administration
- Plant Operations
- Business Operations
- Technology Operations
- Central and Board Operations

In this format, all accounts that are used to record regular education expenses are listed as a group, all accounts that are used to record special education expenses are listed together, and so forth.

The accounts under each functional area are used to record both personnel and non-personnel expenses associated with those areas. For example, personnel expense accounts that might be used for regular education teachers might include:

- Regular Education Teacher Salaries
- Regular Education Teacher FICA
- Regular Education Teacher Pensions
- Regular Education Teacher Health Insurance
- Regular Education Teacher Workers' Compensation Insurance
- Regular Education Teacher Unemployment Compensation Insurance

Non-personnel expense accounts under each functional area are typically broken down into categories to enhance the overall organization of the accounts, for example:

- Contracted Services
- Travel
- Supplies and Equipment
- Dues and Fees
- Other Non-Personnel Expenses

The following are examples of accounts that might appear under various functional areas:

Regular Education
- Regular Education Teacher Salaries
- Substitute Pay
- Accounts for each benefit provided to regular education teachers and substitutes (FICA, pensions, health insurance, workers' compensation insurance, and unemployment compensation insurance)
- Accounts for regular education contracted services, travel, supplies expense, equipment expense, and dues and fees
- Regular Education Tuition
- Regular Education Field Trips

Ancillary Student Services
- Bus Driver Wages
- Accounts for each benefit provided to bus drivers
- Coach Earnings
- Accounts for each benefit provided to coaches
- Accounts for transportation-related contracted services, travel, supplies expense, equipment expense, and dues and fees
- Accounts for athletics-related contracted services, travel, supplies expense, equipment expense, and dues and fees

Plant Operations
- Buildings and Grounds Director Salary
- Maintenance and Custodial Wages

The Budget Layout 47

- Maintenance and Custodial Overtime
- Accounts for each benefit provided to employees working in plant operations
- Accounts for plant operations contracted services, travel, supplies expense, equipment expense, and dues and fees
- Building Repairs and Maintenance
- Building Inspections and Certificates
- Vehicle Inspections
- Electricity
- Water and Sewage
- Natural Gas
- Capital Projects

Business Operations
- Business Administrator Salary
- Business Assistant Salaries
- Accounts for each benefit provided to business office personnel
- Accounts for business office contracted services, travel, supplies expense, equipment expense, and dues and fees
- Audit Fees
- Insurance
- Loan Payments
- Lease Payments
- Tax Refunds

Technology Operations
- Technology Director Salary
- Technology Assistant Wages
- Technology Assistant Overtime
- Accounts for each benefit provided to technology staff
- Accounts for technology department contracted services, travel, supplies expense, equipment expense, and dues and fees

Central and Board Operations
- Superintendent Salary
- Assistant to Superintendent Salary
- Accounts for each benefit provided to central office staff
- Accounts for central office contracted services, travel, supplies expense, equipment expense, and dues and fees
- Legal Retainer
- Other Legal Fees
- Public Relations
- Advertising

These functional areas and accounts are often broken down even further by categories such as building, grade level, or course subject.

Special Education Accounts

The special education functional area can be broken down into the following subgroups:

- Early Intervention
- Emotional Support
- English Language Learner Support
- Extended School Year
- Gifted Support
- Hearing Support
- Learning Support
- Life Skills Support
- Occupational and Physical Therapy
- Speech Language Support
- Vision Support
- Other Special Education Services

The accounts in each subgroup are then organized in a manner similar to those for the other functional areas. Salary and benefit accounts are designated for each special education position in each subgroup, including both teacher and paraprofessional positions, and non-personnel accounts are broken down into the same categories as those previously shown.

Instructional Support Services Accounts

The accounts in the instructional support services area follow a similar pattern and can be divided into the following subgroups:

- Nursing
- Guidance
- Psychology
- Library
- Other Support Services

Educational Administration Accounts

Accounts associated with the administration of educational programs are organized in a similar way. These accounts can be divided into the following subgroups, each with its own set of personnel and non-personnel accounts:

- Curriculum Office
- Special Education Office
- Elementary School Principal
- Secondary School Principal
- Other Educational Administration Offices

Personnel expense accounts in this section of the expenditure budget include those for administrators, their assistants, and any other personnel who may be involved in the administration of educational programs.

DESIGNING THE BUDGET FOR INFORMED DECISIONS

When Pre-Encumbrances Are Available

Each account has its own budget and is used to monitor available balances for the particular type of expenditures for which it is designated. It is important that the balance of each represents the true amount remaining at any point in time so that spending decisions are well informed. This requires factoring planned spending that has not yet occurred into the balance. Some accounting software programs allow for pre-encumbrances, which reserve funds for planned orders and spending before they occur. In this way, if a school district plans to purchase an item but has not ordered it yet, the funds that will be needed for the purchase can be reserved ahead of time through a pre-encumbrance that reduces the available balance of the account.

Consider a situation in which $9,000 has been budgeted under account "Dept. A Supplies Expense" for two required items requested during the budget preparation period. The total spent on supplies for Dept. A has averaged $10,000 in recent years, so $1,000 is added to the account budget for other miscellaneous items that might come up throughout the year. The account budget is then as follows:

Dept. A Supplies Expense: $10,000
Specific item 1: $5,000
Specific item 2: $4,000
Miscellaneous supplies for Dept. A: $1,000

At the beginning of the year, the $9,000 that has been budgeted for items 1 and 2 is reserved through a pre-encumbrance even though the items have not been ordered yet, reducing the available balance of the account to $1,000. An employee then submits a request to purchase a $2,000 item they would like to have, and the request is appropriately denied so that enough funds remain for items 1 and 2.

When Pre-Encumbrances Are Not Available

When pre-encumbrances are not used and the budgets for specific items planned for purchase during the budget preparation period are combined with those for miscellaneous items that are purchased on an as needed basis, account balances can be misleading. In the example presented above, without pre-encumbrances, the account balance would have still been $10,000 at the time the employee made their request, which might then have been unwisely approved, leaving an insufficient balance of $8,000 for the planned purchase of items 1 and 2.

When using an accounting software that does not have a pre-encumbrance feature (i.e., does not allow for reserving funds by reducing the account balance until an official purchase order has been placed), a different approach is required to ensure that all account balances are true reflections of remaining amounts. This approach requires that the costs of specific items requested during the budget preparation period be projected in accounts separate from those for miscellaneous items that will be requested throughout the year. Applying this approach to the preceding example, the budget is adjusted as follows:

Dept. A Supplies Expense: $9,000
Specific item 1: $5,000
Specific item 2: $4,000
Dept. A Misc. Supplies Expense: $1,000

Notice that the projected cost of miscellaneous supplies has been moved to a separate account. Now when the $2,000 spending request is received, the balance of the account for miscellaneous supplies properly conveys that not enough funds are available to approve the request. By modifying the structure of the accounts, the issue caused by the absence of a pre-encumbrance feature was addressed.

Separating accounts for specific items from those for miscellaneous items should be used for both personnel and non-personnel expenses. For example, the salaries, wages, and benefits of specific employees should be budgeted in accounts separate from those used to budget personnel expenses that will be assigned to multiple employees in an unknown fashion (e.g., overtime and substitute costs).

In terms of non-personnel expenses, examples of costs that should be budgeted in accounts designated for specific items include:

- Expenses for specific supply purchases planned during budget preparation
- Costs for planned field trips to known venues
- Tuition for specific students expected to attend outside institutions
- Anticipated membership dues for specific organizations
- Anticipated registration fees for specific conferences
- Annual building permit fees
- Contracted service charges associated with an agreement that extends into the following year
- Costs for planned building repairs, maintenance projects, and capital improvements
- License fees for software that will be purchased
- Debt service and lease payments required in the following year
- Legal retainer fees required in the subsequent year

Non-personnel costs that should be budgeted in accounts designated for miscellaneous spending include:

- Costs of various supplies that are purchased throughout the year
- Costs of field trips that teachers may take
- Tuition for unknown future students
- Registration fees for conferences that employees may attend
- Costs for unknown future repairs
- Fees for miscellaneous legal services falling outside a standard retainer agreement

Using separate accounts for miscellaneous expenses provides enhanced control, but it does have the potential to clutter a district's ledger of accounts. One way to get around this problem is to limit the number of accounts designated for miscellaneous expenses in each functional area. For example, the following accounts might be used to record non-personnel expenses associated with a special education life skills program:

- Life Skills Contracted Services
- Life Skills Travel
- Life Skills Supplies Expense

- Life Skills Equipment Expense
- Life Skills Dues and Fees
- Life Skills Miscellaneous Non-Personnel Expenses

The first five accounts could then be used to budget the costs of specific items requested for the life skills program during the budget preparation period, while the last account could be used to budget for various items that are purchased throughout the year.

ADDING COLUMNS TO DISPLAY HISTORICAL DATA AND STATISTICAL MEASURES

To streamline the process of determining an appropriate budget for each expense account, the historical charges to each should be shown next to the budget amount in the main budget table, as well as statistical measures such as the mean, median, and regression forecast. It is also helpful to include a "Notes" column to record information that is relevant to the account budget.

An example of this format using made-up numbers for account "Dept. A Misc. Supplies Expense" is shown in table 6.1. Notice in the table that data from years 1–5 are used to forecast an amount for year 7. This is because the development of the year 7 budget would presumably occur during year 6, when the data for that year would not yet be finalized.

SUBSIDIARY EXPENDITURE BUDGETS

An expenditure budget consists of personnel and non-personnel expense accounts. This budget should have a minimum of two subsidiary budgets that branch off from it: the subsidiary personnel budget, which is used to record the underlying detail for certain personnel account budgets, and the subsidiary non-personnel budget, which is used to record the detail for certain non-personnel account budgets.

Account	Yr 1	Yr 2	Yr 3	Yr 4	Yr 5	Mean	Median	Yr 7 Regression Forecast	Yr 7 Budget
Dept. A Misc. Supplies Expense	$850	$830	$1,100	$1,000	$900	$936	$900	$1,044	$1,000

Table 6.1. Main Expenditure Budget Layout

Subsidiary Personnel Budget

Personnel expenses that can be attributed to specific employees should be listed in the subsidiary personnel budget, while those that cannot should be projected directly in the main expenditure budget. For instance, the wages of three employees who work in Department A should be listed in the subsidiary budget, while overtime and substitute payments that will be distributed in an unknown fashion to multiple employees should be projected directly in the main budget. This can be illustrated as follows:

Main Expenditure Budget
  Dept. A Wages: $105,000 (from subsidiary budget, $40,000 + $35,000 + $30,000)
  Dept. A Overtime: $5,000 (projected directly in main budget)
  Dept. A Substitutes: $1,000 (projected directly in main budget)
Subsidiary Personnel Budget:
  Dept. A Employee 1 Wages: $40,000
  Dept. A Employee 2 Wages: $35,000
  Dept. A Employee 3 Wages: $30,000

Personnel expenses include not just employee compensation but also benefits. An effective way to design a subsidiary personnel budget table is to list one position and employee in each row and amounts for their compensation and benefits in adjacent columns. It is also helpful to include columns to indicate whether a position is considered essential or expendable and to show the expenditure accounts to which the amounts are assigned. As with the main budget, a column for notes is also helpful. Table 6.2 shows an abbreviated version of this format assuming a pension rate of 10 percent and using made-up costs for health insurance and workers' compensation insurance.

Just as the total compensation of Department A employees 1–3 from the subsidiary budget is the budget for account "Dept. A Wages" in the main expenditure budget, the total of each of their benefits from the subsidiary

Position/ Employee	Sal/Wage	FICA	Pension	Health Ins	WC Ins	UC Ins	Total	Essential/ Expendable
Position/ Employee1	$40,000	$3,060	$4,000	$18,000	$163	$42	$65,265	Essential
Position/ Employee2	$35,000	$2,678	$3,500	$16,000	$142	$42	$57,362	Essential
Position/ Employee3	$30,000	$2,295	$3,000	$8,000	$122	$42	$43,459	Essential

Table 6.2. Subsidiary Personnel Budget Layout

budget must also be assigned to an account in the main budget. Applying the data in table 6.2, the main expenditure budget is expanded as follows:

Main Expenditure Budget
Dept. A Wages: $105,000 ($40,000 + $35,000 + $30,000)
Dept. A FICA: $8,033 ($3,060 + $2,678 + $2,295)
Dept. A Pensions: $10,500 ($4,000 + $3,500 + $3,000)
Dept. A Health Insurance: $42,000 ($18,000 + $16,000 + $8,000)
Dept. A Workers' Compensation Insurance: $427 ($163 + $142 + $122)
Dept. A Unemployment Compensation Insurance: $126 ($42 + $42 + $42)
Dept. A Overtime: $5,000
Dept. A Substitutes: $1,000

Subsidiary Non-Personnel Budget

As with personnel accounts, some non-personnel accounts should be designated for specific items, while others should be designated for miscellaneous items. Just as personnel costs that are attributable to specific employees should be listed in a subsidiary budget, so too should costs for identifiable non-personnel items. Costs for miscellaneous non-personnel items, on the other hand, should be estimated directly in the main expenditure budget. For example, one supply account budget might represent the cost of a computer and printer for Department A, while another might represent the estimated cost of miscellaneous consumable supplies for that department:

Main Expenditure Budget
  Dept. A Supplies Expense: $1,900 (from subsidiary budget, $1,000 + $900)
  Dept. A Misc. Supplies Expense: $500 (projected directly in main budget)
Subsidiary Non-Personnel Budget
  Computer for Dept. A: $1,000
  Printer for Dept. A: $900

A fully designed subsidiary non-personnel budget table should list item descriptions, vendors from which the items will be purchased, quantities, unit prices, and total costs in adjacent columns. It is also advisable to include columns to label items as required or discretionary, to designate the expenditure accounts to which costs are to be assigned, and to take notes. An illustration is shown in table 6.3.

The Budget Layout 55

REVENUE BUDGET LAYOUT

The layout of the revenue budget tends to be much simpler, consisting of fewer accounts that generally do not contain as much underlying detail. The revenue budget is normally divided into three sections: one containing accounts that are used to record local sources of revenue, another for state sources, and a third for federal sources. A sample layout might look like this:

Local Revenues
- Property Tax
- Income Tax
- Sales Tax
- Interest Earnings
- Admission Fees
- Rental Proceeds
- Advertising Proceeds
- Local Grant A
- Local Grant B
- Miscellaneous Local Revenues

State Revenues
- Regular Education Subsidy
- Special Education Subsidy
- Student Transportation Subsidy
- Student Health Services Subsidy
- Tuition Cost Reimbursement
- FICA Cost Reimbursement
- Pension Cost Reimbursement
- Debt Service Reimbursement
- State Grant A
- State Grant B
- Miscellaneous State Revenue

Federal Revenues
- Title I Grant

Item Description	Vendor	Quantity	Unit Price	Total Cost	Expense Account	Required/Discretionary
Computer for Dept. A	Vendor name	1	$1,000	$1,000	Dept. A Supplies Expense	Discretionary
Printer for Dept. A	Vendor name	1	$900	$900	Dept. A Supplies Expense	Discretionary

Table 6.3. Subsidiary Non-personnel Budget Layout

- Title II Grant
- Title III Grant
- Title IV Grant
- IDEA Grant
- Other Federal Grants

Chapter 7

The Budgeting Process

This book began with an explanation of general budgeting applications and techniques. It then shifted its focus to school district operations, the costs they entail, and the revenue sources that fund them. Next, techniques and methods for projecting school district costs and revenues as part of the budgeting process were presented. This chapter discusses the ongoing nature of this process and outlines its major stages.

RECORDING INFORMATION ON AN ONGOING BASIS

Most school districts have a fiscal year that runs from July through June, so their budgets must be finalized by no later than June 30 each year. This might seem to indicate that a good time for districts to begin the budgeting process would be sometime in January. While it is true that the process ramps up at about this time, some parts of it should begin much sooner. This is because information that is relevant to the budget can materialize at any point and should be recorded on an ongoing basis as it is learned. The main budget and subsidiary budget tables should be set up and ready for use throughout the entire year so that information can be recorded in those tables whenever necessary. Using this approach maximizes efficiency and helps to avoid mistakes and oversights that might otherwise result by waiting until later to begin compiling budgetary information.

An example of an item that might be relevant to the budget is a purchase request from a technology director for a software license. If the request is approved and the license is likely to be renewed annually going forward, pertinent information about the license should be recorded in the subsidiary non-personnel budget table at the time of approval so that it is easily accessible and is not overlooked later. Another example is a notice from a facilities director that new building equipment that was just installed will need to be inspected annually by an outside company. This information should be noted immediately in the subsidiary budget table. Yet another example is a notice from an employee that they will be retiring at the end of the fiscal year. In this case, a note should be added to the subsidiary personnel budget table.

Information pertaining to newly negotiated contracts or newly hired employees should also be recorded as it is learned. Tables 7.1 and 7.2 demonstrate what the preceding notations might look like in abbreviated tables.

BUDGETING STAGES

As information is gleaned and recorded in the main and subsidiary budget tables, a parallel set of budget development procedures that start a bit later in the year should also occur. Some of these are technical in nature, involving data input and quantitative analysis, while others focus primarily on communication and collaboration. While a budget is a technical document, it is shaped based on the input of many individuals, such as board members, administrators, teachers, and other employees and stakeholders. There are six general stages of the budget development process, each of which is discussed in a subsequent chapter of this book:

1. Establish Goals, Parameters, and Plans (chapter 9)
2. Develop the Personnel Budget (chapter 10)
3. Develop the Non-Personnel Budget (chapter 11)
4. Budget Miscellaneous Expenses and Add Contingency Allowance (chapter 12)
5. Budget Revenues (chapter 13)
6. Meet, Make Adjustments, and Finalize Budget (chapter 14)

While this sequence is ideal, the stages do not necessarily have to occur in the exact order shown.

Item Description	Vendor	Expense Account	Required/ Discretionary	Note
License for software	ABC Co.	Technology Operations Software	Discretionary	License fee recurs annually. Year 1 cost: $500
Inspection fee for new building equipment	DEF Co.	Building Inspections and Certificates	Required	Inspection required every year
Educational services contract	GHI Co.	Regular Instruction Contracted Services	Discretionary	Agreement entered into 08/10/202x. Initial year cost: $2,000 per month

Table 7.1. Subsidiary Non-personnel Budget Notations

Position	Employee	Sal/Wage	FICA	Essential/Expendable	Note
Teacher	Jones, Mary			Essential	Employee retiring at end of year
Teacher	Smith, John			Essential	Employee hired 01/15/202x.. Starting salary: $50,000

Table 7.2. Subsidiary Personnel Budget Notations

Chapter 8 will describe a hypothetical school district that will be used to illustrate the application of budgeting procedures recommended in chapters 9 through 14.

Chapter 8

Small Town School District

To illustrate the steps involved in developing a school district budget, the hypothetical Small Town School District will be used as an example. Small Town School District's stated values are as follows:

1. Safety, Fairness, and Respect
2. Exceptional Academic Programs
3. Outstanding Arts Programs
4. Strong Image

The characteristics and features of Small Town School District are described in this chapter.

EXPENSES

Buildings and Equipment

Small Town School District consists of an elementary school and a high school. An annual permit fee of $100 must be paid for each building, and each has an alarm system consisting of card readers, cameras, security software, and other components. The district has an agreement with an outside company that monitors its alarm systems on an ongoing basis for a monthly fee of $500. In addition, the HVAC systems in the two buildings are covered by a preventive maintenance agreement with an outside vendor that requires quarterly payments of $9,000. Both of these agreements expire in five years.

Utilities for each building include electricity, water and sewage, and natural gas. Contracted services are used for general repairs and maintenance such as plumbing and electrical work, and more extensive capital projects are periodically undertaken to renovate the buildings. Additionally, the district has three vehicles that are required to undergo annual state inspections that typically cost about $1,000 each.

Plant Operations

Small Town School District employs twelve full-time unionized custodians who take care of the buildings and grounds. These individuals are paid an hourly wage for eight hours per day, 260 days per year. Their average regular rate of pay will be $18.27 per hour in the upcoming year, based on a collective bargaining agreement with the district, and they are also expected to work overtime as needed.

Educational Programs and Student Support Services

Small Town School District offers both regular and special education programs for students. Learning support services are offered in-house, while all other special education services are provided by outside contractors or schools that charge fees or tuition.

There are 101 regular education teachers employed by the district, one of whom is paid through a federal Title I grant. There are also ten learning support teachers. All teachers are union members who are paid an annual salary that is determined according to negotiated salary schedules that extend into the following year. The average salary of the non-grant-funded regular education teachers will be $59,400 in the upcoming year, while the salary of the Title I teacher will be $70,000. The average salary of the learning support teachers will be $65,000.

The schedules base each teacher's salary on their experience and educational credentials. First-year teachers with a bachelor's degree will be paid $50,000 in the upcoming year, while those with a master's degree will be paid $53,000. There are also fifteen paraprofessionals who will earn $18.21 per hour on average for 7.5 hours per day over 183 days.

The district also provides student support services, including a nurse and a guidance counselor at each building. Each nurse will be paid a salary of $70,000, while the elementary school guidance counselor and high school guidance counselor will earn $64,000 and $63,000, respectively.

Ancillary Services

Student transportation is provided by an outside bus company with which the district has an agreement that extends into the following year. Transportation billings are based on the number of runs and the rates for the vehicles assigned to those runs. The total annual cost of the billings has been steadily increasing in recent years and is expected to reach approximately $2,000,000 in the upcoming year.

The district also provides students with opportunities to participate in sports. In the upcoming year, four coaches will be paid an annual stipend of $3,000 each through the district's payroll.

Administration

Small Town School District is led by a volunteer board of directors and a paid administrative team. In addition to the superintendent, there are seven other administrators. Each is covered under an employment agreement that spells out their compensation in the following year. The administrators and their salaries in that year will be:

- Superintendent ($150,000)
- Finance director ($120,000)
- Curriculum director ($115,000)
- Special education director ($105,000)
- High school principal ($100,000)
- Elementary school principal ($95,000)
- Buildings and grounds director ($80,000)
- Technology director ($80,000)

Each administrator, except the finance director and buildings and grounds director, has one assistant. The finance director, who oversees all business-related functions and prepares the district budget, has two assistants: one handles accounts payable, accounts receivable, purchasing, and receiving, and the other handles human resources and payroll functions. The buildings and grounds director, who manages the custodial staff, does not have an assistant. Each assistant is paid an annual salary that has been predetermined for the upcoming year, and those salaries will range from $39,000 to $52,000.

Each administrator is responsible for managing operations and spending in their area and in several cases an additional area as well. For instance, the superintendent also handles public relations and advertising, and the curriculum director oversees instructional support services. The special education director coordinates transportation with the district's contracted transportation provider, and the high school principal manages the district's athletic programs. The elementary school principal also serves as the district's federal grants manager.

Employee Benefits

The district provides the following benefits to employees:

- FICA contributions
- Pension contributions
- Health insurance
- Workers' compensation insurance
- Federal unemployment compensation insurance

These benefits are offered to all employees, with the exception of coaches, who are not offered health insurance.

The employer pension contribution rate for the upcoming year has not yet been certified, but according to the most recent actuarial reports that have been published, the rate is projected to be around 9 percent. Employees may select among the following health insurance coverage levels, with annual rates that are currently as follows:

- Individual ($8,224)
- Employee-Spouse ($15,421)
- Family ($19,533)

Of the one hundred non-grant-funded regular education teachers, nine have individual coverage, twenty have employee-spouse coverage, seventy have family coverage, and one does not take any coverage. The Title I teacher has family coverage. Of the ten learning support teachers, two have employee-spouse coverage and eight have family coverage. Of the fifteen paraprofessionals, two have individual coverage, four have employee-spouse coverage, and nine have family coverage. Of the twelve custodians, two have individual coverage, four have employee-spouse coverage, and six have family coverage. In addition, the following coverages apply to the district's other employees:

- *Family Coverage*: superintendent, finance director, special education director, buildings and grounds director, high school principal, 1st assistant to finance director, assistant to curriculum director, assistant to high school principal, assistant to elementary school principal, elementary school nurse, high school nurse, elementary guidance counselor
- *Employee-Spouse Coverage*: curriculum director, elementary school principal, 2nd assistant to finance director, high school guidance counselor
- *Individual Coverage*: technology director, assistant to superintendent, assistant to special education director, assistant to technology director

Increases in the cost of health insurance have fluctuated between 5 and 10 percent in recent years, with an average rate increase of 7 percent. The cost of workers' compensation insurance has been between $35,000 and $42,000 over the past several years, with a slight but consistent upward trend during that period.

Loans and Leases

Small Town School District has one outstanding bank loan and leases its copiers and postage machines. The loan requires an annual debt service payment of $350,000 in each of the next ten years. The leases each cover sixty months and began one year ago, with the copiers leased for $7,000 per month and the postage machines leased for $400 per month.

Legal and Accounting Services

The district is represented by outside legal counsel and is in the first year of a five-year agreement with a firm that conducts annual audits of its financial statements and records as required by law. A monthly retainer of $1,000 is paid in relation to the legal agreement, and additional fees apply for services falling outside the standard scope of the agreement. The district has been informed by its attorney that the retainer fee will remain flat in the upcoming year. The audit fee is billed in four equal installments and will be a total of $20,000 in the upcoming year.

District Insurance

District insurance policies are purchased through the district's insurance broker and include property, auto, and cyber insurance. Respective costs for each in the current year are $50,000, $5,000, and $15,000. The annual cost of insurance has been rising at a rate of about 3 percent in recent years, and quotes have not yet been received for the upcoming year.

Software

Software products used by Small Town School District include curriculum mapping, device monitoring, and financial programs. The first of these is used by the curriculum director, the second by the technology director, and the third by the finance director. While the annual cost of the financial software is locked in at $25,000 for the next three years, the costs of the other two programs in the upcoming year are still being researched by the curriculum director and technology director.

REVENUES

Local Taxes

Small Town School District levies property taxes as its main source of local revenue, and its property tax rate is 21.4 mills. The taxes levied against properties are based on their assessments on the first day of the fiscal year, and property tax collection rates are typically around 95 percent of the amount billed. (At times, property taxes must be refunded due to overpayments or assessment reductions, and when this occurs, the refunds are recorded as expenses.)

Property taxes that are not collected in the year in which they are levied are pursued through a delinquent tax collection program. Delinquent collections in each of the past several years have been between 3 and 7 percent of current collections.

Property assessment information is provided by the county in which the district is located. According to the county website, the total assessment of all properties located in the district is currently $642,386,121. There is a new commercial development in progress that is expected to be assessed at approximately $10,000,000 and added to the assessment rolls prior to the beginning of the upcoming year.

The district also charges income tax. Income tax revenues have risen steadily over the past five years, with collections as follows:

- 5 years ago: $1,660,299
- 4 years ago: $1,716,713
- 3 years ago: $1,810,542
- 2 years ago: $1,927,475
- 1 year ago: $2,027,472

Investment Income

Small Town School District has $2,000,000 invested in a savings account that offers an effective interest rate of 3.25 percent. The latest economic forecasts suggest that rates will remain steady for the foreseeable future.

Other Local Revenues

Other local revenues include admission fees paid by event attendees, proceeds from renting out facilities to community groups and other organizations, and website advertising fees. Admission fees typically bring in about $30,000 per year, and rental proceeds are usually around $17,000. Website advertising fees have steadily increased since they were instituted five years ago, from $4,036 in the first year to $15,089 one year ago.

State Subsidies and Federal Grants

The district receives state subsidies for basic education, special education, student transportation, and student health services. As noted earlier, it also receives an annual Title I award from the federal government that is used to pay for one regular education teacher's salary and benefits. The professional school business association to which the finance director belongs estimates that the district's state subsidies will be as follows in the upcoming year:

- Basic Education Subsidy: $3,290,000
- Special Education Subsidy: $712,500
- Student Transportation Services Subsidy: $436,000
- Student Health Services Subsidy: $18,745

The district's federal grants manager estimates that the Title I grant amount will be $104,000.

ACCOUNTING SYSTEM LAYOUT

Expenditure Accounts

Small Town School District's accounting system does not have a pre-encumbrance feature, and its expense accounts are broken down into the following functional areas:

- Regular Instruction
- Special Education
- Educational Administration
- Instructional Support Services
- Ancillary Student Services
- Plant Operations
- Business Operations
- Technology Operations
- Central and Board Operations

Each area contains accounts that are used to forecast and track the costs of employees falling in that category, as well as accounts to track the following types of non-personnel expenses:

- Contracted service charges
- Employee travel costs
- Supplies expenses
- Equipment expenses
- Dues and fees

Where appropriate, two separate accounts exist to track the same type of expense: one to track spending on specific items requested during the budget preparation period and another to track spending on miscellaneous items that are purchased as needed throughout the year. Additionally, the following expense accounts exist under the functional areas shown:

Regular Instruction
- Regular Instruction Books Expense
- Regular Instruction Field Trips

Special Education
- Special Education Tuition

Educational Administration
- Curriculum Software Expense

Plant Operations
- Building Repairs and Maintenance
- Building Inspections and Certificates
- Vehicle Inspections
- Electricity
- Water and Sewage
- Natural Gas
- Capital Projects

Business Operations
- Financial Software Expense
- Audit Fees
- District Insurance
- Loan Payments
- Lease Payments
- Tax Refunds

Technology Operations
- Technology Software Expense

Central and Board Operations
- Legal Retainer
- Public Relations and Advertising

REVENUE ACCOUNTS

The district's revenue accounts are as follows:

- Property Tax Revenue
- Income Tax Revenue
- Delinquent Property Tax Revenue
- Investment Income
- Admission Fees
- Rental Proceeds
- Website Advertising Fees
- Basic Education Subsidy
- Special Education Subsidy
- Student Transportation Services Subsidy
- Student Health Services Subsidy
- Title I Grant Revenue

Chapter 9

Stage 1
Establish Goals, Parameters, and Plans

A recommended first step in the budgeting process is for the school board (or a committee of the board) to meet to go over the budgeting process and establish strategic goals and parameters for the upcoming year. The guidance the board provides should focus on the "big picture" and reflect the priorities of the community at large. Because board members typically do not have an intricate knowledge of school district finances and operations, district administrators such as the superintendent and business administrator should also be in attendance to facilitate the discussion by providing background information, answering questions, and making recommendations. It is also possible to include other stakeholders—such as community members, students, teachers, and other employees—in the discussion so that a wider range of perspectives is heard, but it is important to keep in mind that the group must be kept to a manageable size. Once goals and parameters are established, the administrative team should meet to develop tentative plans of action to achieve them.

REVIEW BUDGET APPLICATIONS, PRINCIPLES, AND TIMELINE

The administration should lead off the discussion with the board by explaining what a budget is and how it is used for planning, control, and assessment. The importance of budget accuracy and how it is achieved through a moderate forecasting approach that is neither too aggressive nor too cautious should be explained. Some of the challenges of school district budgeting, such as the unpredictability of special education costs and the complexity of state funding formulas, should be highlighted, as should the collaborative nature of the budgeting process and the role that all employees play in the development of a sound budget.

In addition, the budgeting process and timeline should be reviewed. Everyone should understand key dates such as submission deadlines and scheduled meetings pertaining to the budget and at which various drafts of the budget will be presented.

ESTABLISH GOALS AND PARAMETERS

Assess the District's Performance and Define Goals

Next, the board should think about the district's values and its strengths and weaknesses in the context of those values in order to identify areas for improvement. Existing opportunities and challenges as well as ways to respond to them should also be considered. To facilitate this part of the discussion, the administration should provide a status update, going over financial results in recent years, any trends that may exist, and the district's present financial condition. Updates on academic and programmatic outcomes should also be provided. Benchmarking data that compare the district's performance in various areas to that of its peers can also provide insight.

Based on the results of the analysis, strategic goals can be developed.

ESTABLISH FINANCIAL PARAMETERS

Once goals have been established, the next step is for the board to establish financial parameters within which the administration should work in developing a plan to achieve the stated goals. As an example, the board might stipulate that the budget can project a deficit no greater than a certain amount. The financial parameters that are imposed should be realistic, accounting for past performance and the ambitiousness of the goals that have been set, among other factors. Other items that should be addressed are the amount of the contingency allowance that should be budgeted and the maximum tax increase that would be considered.

IDENTIFY CUT OPTIONS

In order to develop a plan to achieve the board's stated goals within the financial parameters that have been stipulated, the administration may have to cut expenses from the budget. To provide guidance to the administration as it carries out its work, the board should communicate whether any existing programs or positions can be cut if necessary. For instance, the board might state a maximum number of teaching positions that can be eliminated if necessary.

An important role administrators play in this part of the board's deliberations is to make sure that each board member is fully aware of the potential ramifications of any cuts that might be made. As an example, a decision to furlough teachers could lead to increased class sizes, a decline in student performance, harm to the district's reputation, employee disgruntlement, and so on.

DEVELOP PLANS

After the board has established its goals and guidelines, the next step is for the district administrators to meet to:

- Narrow the goals if necessary to focus on the most pressing issues
- Develop ideas to achieve each goal
- Formulate tentative action plans that can realistically be accomplished within the next year
- Make rough estimates of action plan costs to include in the initial version of the budget

As the chief executive officer, the superintendent may wish to direct these meetings. It is also a good idea for the district business administrator to be in attendance to:

- Comment on the financial implications of any ideas that are being discussed
- Be aware of the budgetary effects of any decisions that are made
- Assist with forming cost estimates

Other administrators can limit their attendance to those meetings where the specific area(s) they oversee will be a focal point.

SMALL TOWN SCHOOL DISTRICT

The following is Small Town School District's application of the previous steps.

Assess the District's Performance and Define Goals

As a first step, the school board reviews the district's values, which are:

1. Safety, Fairness, and Respect
2. Exceptional Academic Programs
3. Outstanding Arts Programs
4. Strong Image

The district's strengths and weaknesses in the context of these values are then considered. Regarding the first value, a determination is made that building security needs to be improved because there have been two reported cases of unauthorized persons in the buildings in the past year. Regarding the second value, the board feels there is room for improvement in academic outcomes based on benchmarking data that have been presented by the administration. Regarding the third value, the board does not identify any weaknesses but does note that it would like the district's theater arts program to receive more recognition. Regarding the fourth value, several board members comment that the buildings are aging and beginning to look run down. They also note that the buildings' HVAC systems are outdated. The following strategic goals are agreed upon to address the weaknesses that have been identified:

1. Increase building security
2. Raise standardized test scores and college acceptance rates
3. Renovate and update buildings

Establish Financial Parameters

The school board then decides to stipulate that the budget include a contingency allowance of 1 percent of budgeted expenses and that projected revenues be equal to or greater than the total combined amount of budgeted expenses and the contingency allowance. It also indicates a willingness to consider a property tax rate increase of up to 2 percent.

Identify Cut Options

Next, the board contemplates whether there are any existing programs or positions it would be open to cutting in order to stay within the financial parameters it has established. The board ultimately decides that it does not wish to make any cuts in these areas.

Develop Plans

Based on the outcomes of the board discussion, Small Town School District's administrative team decides to schedule one meeting to develop ideas and tentative action plans for each goal the board has set. The following are the team's notes from each meeting.

Meeting to Discuss Strategic Goal 1: Increase building security
- Administrators in Attendance: superintendent, finance director, buildings and grounds director, high school principal, elementary school principal, technology director
- Ideas
  - Hire security guards
  - Add cameras
  - Install new security software and card readers
  - Add security vestibule at each main entrance
- Tentative Action Plans Selected and Cost Estimate to Include in Initial Version of Budget
  - Install new security software and card readers (cost estimate: $15,000)

Meeting to Discuss Strategic Goal 2: Raise standardized test scores and college acceptance rates
- Administrators in Attendance: superintendent, finance director, curriculum director, special education director, high school principal, elementary school principal
- Narrowed Goal for Upcoming Year
  - Raise math test scores
- Ideas
  - Purchase new math curriculum
  - Hire additional math teacher
  - Add hourly supplemental math tutoring position to be filled by an existing teacher
  - Increase monitoring of student metrics and student interventions
- Tentative Action Plans Selected and Cost Estimates to Include in Initial Version of Budget
  - Hire additional math teacher who has a master's degree (cost estimate: $83,032)
  - Add supplemental math tutoring position for which pay will have to be negotiated (cost estimate: $15,230)

Meeting to Discuss Strategic Goal 3: Renovate and update buildings
- Administrators in Attendance: superintendent, finance director, buildings and grounds director, high school principal, elementary school principal, technology director
- Ideas
  - Repair and restore building facades
  - Install new building control system to improve air quality, flow, and temperature control
  - Install new network switches to improve internet connectivity and network speeds
  - Upgrade theater sound system
  - Consult with outside architects and engineers to identify ways to modernize buildings and develop capital projects schedule
- Tentative Action Plan and Cost Estimate Selected to Include in Initial Version of Budget
  - Install new building control system (cost estimate: $500,000)
  - Upgrade theater sound system (cost estimate: $30,000)

Chapter 10

Stage 2
Develop the Personnel Budget

The development of a school district budget is normally handled by a business administrator, who may do the actual work of preparing the budget, oversee budget preparation tasks performed by assistants, or a combination of both. A major step in developing a school district budget is to project personnel expenses, which include employee compensation and benefits. As stated previously, it is recommended that those personnel expenses that can be tied to specific employees be projected in a subsidiary personnel budget that branches off from the main expenditure budget. This chapter describes the basic steps to developing the personnel budget.

STEPS FOR DEVELOPING PERSONNEL BUDGET

Step 1: Form a List of Positions and Employees

The first step in developing the personnel budget is to list all positions and employees. If any positions are or will become vacant, a note such as "To Be Determined (TBD)" should be entered in the employee name field. The list should also reflect any pending employee transfers and plans to add or eliminate positions.

Step 2: Budget Employee Compensation

Once the initial list of positions and employees is complete, the next step is to review any CBAs, employment contracts, addenda, or other related documents to determine the amount each employee will earn in the upcoming year. Earnings can be in the form of salaries, wages, stipends, and bonuses, among other possibilities.

If there are employees who are in a CBA that is set to expire before the start of the upcoming year and for whom a new agreement has not yet been negotiated, those employees' raises and earnings will have to be estimated until a new agreement has been adopted. Being involved in the negotiation process and knowing the positions of the negotiating parties can help to provide insight into what estimates to make. The earnings of future employees who will fill vacant positions may have to be approximated as well. As an example, the salary of a yet-to-be-identified teacher to fill an open position will be uncertain if their salary will depend on their educational credentials.

Step 3: Budget Employee Benefits

After employee compensation has been budgeted, employee benefits should be budgeted. Based on existing laws at the time of this writing, the projected cost of employer FICA contributions for employees earning $147,000 or less should be 7.65 percent of their projected earnings, and the projected cost of federal unemployment compensation insurance should be 0.6 percent of their first $7,000 of projected earnings. The amount to budget for state unemployment compensation insurance varies by state.

Benefits such as pensions, health insurance, and workers' compensation insurance should also be budgeted. Some or all of these may have to be estimated at this stage, depending on the information that is currently available. For example, if the state pension rate for the upcoming year has not yet been certified, an estimate of that rate will be necessary until the official rate is published. Actuarial reports on public school employee retirement systems can often be used as a basis for such an estimate when necessary.

If quotes for employee insurance have not been received or employees have not had an opportunity to make their coverage selections for the upcoming year, it will be necessary to estimate future insurance premiums until quotes are received and accepted. A reasonable approach is to assume that employee coverage selections will remain the same as they are currently (unless information to the contrary is known) and to estimate an increase to the current year premiums based on past trends. A district's claims history and pricing trends in the general insurance market should also be considered when making the estimate, and consulting with a district's insurance broker is always a good idea.

Step 4: Calculate the Total Cost of Each Position and All Positions Combined

Next, the total compensation and benefits of each position should be calculated.

Step 5: Label Each Position as Essential or Expendable

The fifth step in developing the personnel budget is to classify each position as essential or expendable. This will help simplify the process of cutting expenses from the budget later if this becomes necessary to meet a financial goal.

Step 6: Tie Amounts from Steps 2 and 3 to Expense Accounts

Finally, each compensation and benefit amount that has been listed should be assigned to one or more expense accounts from the main expenditure budget. The total assigned to each account then becomes part of the overall budget for the functional area, department, or building for which it is designated.

HIGHLIGHTING ESTIMATES THAT MAY STILL BE ADJUSTED

If there are projections in the personnel budget that are estimates, it is likely that some will be refined over time as more information becomes available. Following the examples described above, when a CBA that was being negotiated at the time the budget was first created is settled, bargaining unit member earnings prescribed by the terms of the new agreement can replace the initial estimates of those amounts. Similarly, when a teacher is hired to fill a vacant position for which the salary was initially estimated, the actual starting salary can replace the estimate. When a state pension system certifies its employer contribution rate for the upcoming year, the estimated rate can be replaced by the official rate. Finally, when insurance quotes are received and accepted, they can take the place of the estimated premiums that were temporarily budgeted.

As estimates are made in the personnel budget, it is important to call attention to those that may still be refined later by highlighting or labeling them or displaying them in a different font or color.

SMALL TOWN SCHOOL DISTRICT

Steps 1–5

Figure 10.1 is an abbreviated version of Small Town School District's personnel budget after applying steps 1–5. This has been developed based on the

Chapter 10

SUBSIDIARY PERSONNEL BUDGET
Small Town School District

Position	Sal/Wage	FICA	Pension	Health Ins	WC Ins	UC Ins	Total	Ess/Exp
Superintendent	$ 150,000	$ 11,289	$ 13,500	$ 20,900	$ 750	$ 42	$ 196,481	Essential
Finance Director	$ 120,000	$ 9,180	$ 10,800	$ 20,900	$ 600	$ 42	$ 161,522	Essential
Curriculum Director	$ 115,000	$ 8,798	$ 10,350	$ 16,500	$ 575	$ 42	$ 151,265	Essential
Special Education Director	$ 105,000	$ 8,033	$ 9,450	$ 20,900	$ 525	$ 42	$ 143,950	Essential
High School Principal	$ 100,000	$ 7,650	$ 9,000	$ 20,900	$ 500	$ 42	$ 138,092	Essential
Ele School Principal	$ 95,000	$ 7,268	$ 8,550	$ 16,500	$ 475	$ 42	$ 127,835	Essential
B & G Director	$ 80,000	$ 6,120	$ 7,200	$ 20,900	$ 400	$ 42	$ 114,662	Essential
Technology Director	$ 80,000	$ 6,120	$ 7,200	$ 8,800	$ 400	$ 42	$ 102,562	Essential
Asst to Superintendent	$ 52,000	$ 3,978	$ 4,680	$ 8,800	$ 260	$ 42	$ 69,760	Essential
1st Asst to Finance Dir	$ 50,000	$ 3,825	$ 4,500	$ 20,900	$ 250	$ 42	$ 79,517	Essential
2nd Asst to Finance Dir	$ 50,000	$ 3,825	$ 4,500	$ 16,500	$ 250	$ 42	$ 75,117	Essential
Asst to Curriculum Dir	$ 41,600	$ 3,182	$ 3,744	$ 20,900	$ 208	$ 42	$ 69,676	Essential
Asst to Special Ed Director	$ 42,800	$ 3,274	$ 3,852	$ 8,800	$ 214	$ 42	$ 58,982	Essential
Asst to HS Principal	$ 40,000	$ 3,060	$ 3,600	$ 20,900	$ 200	$ 42	$ 67,802	Essential
Asst to Ele School Principal	$ 39,000	$ 2,984	$ 3,510	$ 20,900	$ 195	$ 42	$ 66,631	Essential
Asst to Technology Director	$ 45,000	$ 3,443	$ 4,050	$ 8,800	$ 225	$ 42	$ 61,560	Essential
Regular Ed Teachers 1-100	$ 5,940,000	$ 454,410	$ 534,600	$ 1,872,200	$ 29,700	$ 4,200	$ 8,835,110	Essential
Title I Teacher	$ 70,000	$ 5,355	$ 6,300	$ 20,900	$ 350	$ 42	$ 102,947	Essential
Learn Supp Teachers 1-10	$ 650,000	$ 49,725	$ 58,500	$ 200,200	$ 3,250	$ 420	$ 962,095	Essential
Paraprofessionals 1-15	$ 374,898	$ 28,680	$ 33,741	$ 271,700	$ 1,874	$ 630	$ 711,523	Essential
Ele School Nurse	$ 70,000	$ 5,355	$ 6,300	$ 20,900	$ 350	$ 42	$ 102,947	Essential
High School Nurse	$ 70,000	$ 5,355	$ 6,300	$ 20,900	$ 350	$ 42	$ 102,947	Essential
Ele Guidance Counselor	$ 64,000	$ 4,896	$ 5,760	$ 20,900	$ 320	$ 42	$ 95,918	Essential
HS Guidance Counselor	$ 63,000	$ 4,820	$ 5,670	$ 16,500	$ 315	$ 42	$ 90,347	Essential
Custodians 1-12	$ 456,019	$ 34,885	$ 41,042	$ 209,000	$ 2,280	$ 504	$ 743,730	Essential
Coaches 1-4	$ 12,000	$ 918	$ 1,080	$ -	$ 60	$ 72	$ 14,130	Essential
New Math Teacher	$ 53,000	$ 4,055	$ 4,770	$ 20,900	$ 265	$ 42	$ 83,032	Expendable
New Math Tutor	$ 13,000	$ 995	$ 1,170	$ -	$ 65	$ -	$ 15,230	Expendable

$ 45,207 $ 13,545,370

Step 1. Form a List of Positions and Employees

Step 2. Budget Employee Compensation

Step 3. Budget Employee Benefits

Step 4. Calculate the Total Cost of Each Position and All Positions Combined

Step 5. Label Each Position as Essential or Expendable

Figure 10.1. Small Town School District Subsidiary Personnel Budget

assumption that employees have not yet made their insurance coverage selections for the upcoming year, and the following estimates for that year underlie the amounts shown in the figure:

- Pension rate: 9 percent
- Increase in health insurance premiums: 7 percent
- Total cost of workers' compensation insurance policy: $45,207

The estimated pension rate is in accordance with actuarial reports, and the estimated increase in health insurance premiums matches the average rate increase over the past several years. The estimated cost of workers' compensation insurance reflects the upward trend in this cost in recent years.

Note the following with regard to each column heading:

- **Sal/Wage**: For nearly all positions, salaries and wages are in regular font because the compensation levels for those positions are clearly defined by existing agreements. An exception to this is the projected salary of a new math teacher. This amount is in italics because it is based on assumptions that the position will be approved and that the teacher who fills it will have a master's degree. (Recall from chapter 8 that first-year teachers with a master's degree will earn $53,000 in the upcoming year.) If either of these assumptions turns out to be incorrect, the amount will need to be changed. The compensation for a new math tutor is also in italics since it is a tentative estimate. This would be a new position for which the pay would have to be negotiated. The projected earnings of each employee group are calculated as follows:
  - Regular Education Teachers: Total salaries of non-grant-funded teachers 1–100 ($5,940,000) + salary of Title I teacher ($70,000) = $6,010,000
  - Learning Support Teachers: 10 learning support teachers × $65,000 each on average = $650,000
  - Paraprofessionals: 15 paraprofessionals × 183 days per year × 7.5 hours per day × $18.21 per hour = $374,898
  - Custodians: 12 custodians × 260 days per year × 8 hours per day × $18.27 per hour = $456,019
  - Coaches: 4 coaches × $3,000 per coach = $12,000
- **FICA**—For all employees excluding the superintendent, the cost of FICA is calculated using the following formula:

    FICA Contributions = Employee Earnings × 7.65%

    Because the superintendent's earnings exceed the $147,000 limit on earnings that are subject to Social Security tax, the employer FICA contributions made on their behalf are calculated as follows:
  - Social Security Contributions = Employee's Earnings up to $147,000 × 6.2% = $147,000 × 6.2% = $9,114
  - Medicare Contributions = Employee's Earnings × 1.45% = $150,000 × 1.45% = $2,175
  - FICA Contributions = Social Security Contributions + Medicare Contributions = $9,114 + $2,175 = $11,289
- **Pension**—The cost of each employee's pension is approximated to be 9 percent of their salary to reflect the estimated pension rate. All amounts are shown in italics because they are subject to change pending publication of the official rate.
- **Health Ins**—The amounts listed for health insurance reflect the estimated increase in rates of 7 percent and are calculated as follows:

- Projected rate for individual coverage = Current rate for individual coverage × 1.07 = $8,224 × 1.07 = $8,800
- Projected rate for employee-spouse coverage = Current rate for employee-spouse coverage × 1.07 = $15,421 × 1.07 = $16,500
- Projected rate for family coverage = Current rate for family coverage × 1.07 = $19,533 × 1.07 = $20,900

An assumption has been made that all existing employees will make the same coverage selections for the upcoming year as for the current year and that the new math teacher (if approved) will have family coverage. For those rows where employees are combined, the total cost of health insurance has been calculated as follows:

- Regular Education Teachers: 9 × $8,800 + 20 × $16,500 + 70 × $20,900 + 1 × $0 = $1,872,200
- Learning Support Teachers: 2 × $16,500 + 8 × $20,900 = $200,200
- Paraprofessionals: 2 × $8,800 + 4 × $16,500 + 9 × $20,900 = $271,700
- Custodians: 2 × $8,800 + 4 × $16,500 + 6 × $20,900 = $209,000

The math tutor position does not have a cost for health insurance because as a supplemental position it will be filled by an existing teacher whose health insurance is already budgeted elsewhere, and the coaching positions also do not have this cost since coaches are not covered under the district's health insurance plan. The health insurance projections will continue to be shown in italics until they are replaced by actual quote amounts from a selected insurance provider.
- **WC Ins**—The projected cost of workers' compensation insurance for all employees combined is $45,207, which matches the estimate in figure 10.1. In order to bring about this amount, the cost assigned to each employee has been set at 0.5 percent of their projected earnings. The percentage will be adjusted later as necessary to cause the total cost to match the actual quote that is received and accepted. The numbers will be converted from italics to regular font at that time as well.
- **UC Ins**—The projected cost of federal unemployment compensation insurance for each employee is 0.6 percent of their first $7,000 in earnings. In almost all cases, this is $42, with exceptions for the four coaches and the math tutor position. Since the coaches are expected to earn $3,000 each, the cost of their insurance is projected to be $18 each, and since the math tutor position will be a supplemental position filled by an existing teacher, the cost of their insurance is already budgeted elsewhere.

- **Total**—The total projected cost of each position is shown in italics because it is a function of other estimated amounts that are subject to change. The projected cost of all positions combined in the initial version of the personnel budget is $13,545,370.
- **Ess/Exp**—All existing positions have been labeled as essential because the board previously indicated that it would not be open to eliminating current positions. The new math teacher and tutor positions have been labeled as expendable to convey that they could perhaps be eliminated from the budget if necessary to stay within the required financial parameters.

Step 6

A final step in developing the personnel budget is to assign the amounts in the compensation and benefits columns to expense accounts in the main expenditure budget. Table 10.1 demonstrates what this looks like using column "Sal/Wage" as an example.

Based on the amounts listed in the subsidiary personnel budget and the account assignments, the budget for each account can be determined by calculating the total costs assigned to each. For example, the budgets for the central and business office salary accounts are:

- Central Office Salaries: $150,000 + $52,000 = $202,000
- Business Office Salaries: $120,000 + $50,000 + $50,000 = $220,000

The budgeted costs from the subsidiary personnel budget are then categorized by functional area, and the results are as follows:

- Regular Instruction: Regular education teachers 1–100 ($8,835,110) + Title I teacher ($102,947) + new math teacher ($83,032) + new math tutor ($15,230) = $9,036,319
- Special Education: Learning support teachers 1–10 ($962,095) + paraprofessionals 1–15 ($711,523) = $1,673,618
- Educational Administration: Curriculum director ($151,265) + special education director ($143,950) + high school principal ($138,092) + elementary school principal ($127,835) + assistant to the curriculum director ($69,676) + assistant to the special education director ($58,982) + assistant to the high school principal ($67,802) + assistant to the elementary school principal ($66,631) = $824,233
- Instructional Support Services: Elementary school nurse ($102,947) + high school nurse ($102,947) + elementary guidance counselor ($95,918) + high school guidance counselor ($90,347) = $392,159

PERSONNEL ACCOUNT ASSIGNMENTS
Small Town School District

Position	Sal/Wage	Account
Superintendent	$ 150,000	Central Office Salaries
Finance Director	$ 120,000	Business Office Salaries
Curriculum Director	$ 115,000	Curriculum Office Salaries
Special Education Director	$ 105,000	Special Education Office Salaries
B & G Director	$ 80,000	B & G Director Salary
Technology Director	$ 80,000	Technology Office Salaries
High School Principal	$ 100,000	High School Office Salaries
Ele School Principal	$ 95,000	Ele School Office Salaries
Asst to Superintendent	$ 52,000	Central Office Salaries
1st Asst to Finance Director	$ 50,000	Business Office Salaries
2nd Asst to Finance Director	$ 50,000	Business Office Salaries
Asst to Curriculum Director	$ 41,600	Curriculum Office Salaries
Asst to Special Ed Director	$ 42,800	Special Education Office Salaries
Asst to Technology Director	$ 45,000	Technology Office Salaries
Asst to High School Principal	$ 40,000	High School Office Salaries
Asst to Ele School Principal	$ 39,000	Ele School Office Salaries
Regular Ed Teacher 1-100	$6,000,000	Regular Ed Teacher Salaries
Title I Teacher	$ 70,000	Title I Salary
Learning Support Teachers 1-10	$ 650,000	Learning Support Teacher Salaries
Paraprofessionals 1-15	$ 374,898	Paraprofessional Wages
Ele School Nurse	$ 70,000	Ele School Nurse Salary
High School Nurse	$ 70,000	High School Nurse Salary
Ele School Guidance Counselor	$ 64,000	Ele Guidance Counselor Salary
High School Guidance Counselor	$ 63,000	HS Guidance Counselor Salary
Custodians 1-12	$ 456,019	Custodian Wages
Coaches 1-4	$ 12,000	Coach Stipends
New Math Teacher	$ 53,000	Regular Ed Teacher Salaries
New Math Tutor	$ 13,000	Math Tutor Wages

Table 10.1. Small Town School District Personnel Cost Assignments

- Ancillary Student Services: Coaches 1–4 ($14,130) = $14,130
- Plant Operations: B & G Director ($114,662) + Custodians 1–12 ($743,730) = $858,392
- Business Operations: Finance director ($161,522) + 1st assistant to the finance director ($79,517) + 2nd assistant to the finance director ($75,117) = $316,156
- Technology Operations: Technology director ($102,562) + assistant to the technology director ($61,560) = $164,122
- Central and Board Operations: Superintendent ($196,481) + assistant to the superintendent ($69,760) = $266,241

Chapter 11

Stage 3
Develop the Non-Personnel Budget

In addition to its applications in projecting personnel expenses, a budget is used to project non-personnel expenses. As discussed in chapter 6, it is recommended that non-personnel expenses that can be tied to identifiable items be projected in a subsidiary budget table that contains the following column headings:

- Item Description
- Vendor
- Quantity
- Unit Price
- Total Cost
- Expense Account
- Required/Discretionary
- Note

STEPS FOR DEVELOPING NON-PERSONNEL BUDGET

Step 1: List Required Items and Details in Non-Personnel Budget Table

Items Specified by Contracts

An initial step in completing the non-personnel budget table is to list all known agreements the district is under that extend into the following year and the payments the district will be obligated to make under the terms of those agreements. As the list is compiled, details should be added in adjacent columns such as vendor names, quantities, unit prices, total costs, and so on. Quantities should represent the number of each item that will be purchased or paid for or the number of payments per year required for each item. The total cost of each item should be the product of its quantity and unit price. Agreements that will expire prior to the next fiscal year but are expected to be renewed should be included using estimated costs if they have not yet been renegotiated.

Business administrators are often able to determine appropriate amounts to budget for contracts based on their own knowledge and records. For example, a debt service schedule might tell them how much to budget for payments on a loan, or a lease agreement might indicate how much to budget for lease payments. There are times, however, that assistance from others may be needed to determine how much to budget. For example, a technology director might assist in budgeting the cost of a technology service contract, or a curriculum director might provide pricing information pertaining to an educational services agreement.

Other Required Items

In addition to spending that is contractually obligated, some spending is required by existing laws or regulations. For example, districts are legally required to pay for services for special education students. They may also have to pay building permit fees imposed by the counties in which they are located or vehicle inspection costs required by the state.

Other items may not be legally required but are nonetheless essential. Examples include insurance that provides protection from financial loss and software that is used for critical financial processes.

Step 2: Modify the List Based on Tentative Action Plans

After step 1 is complete, the next step is to modify the list or to add items based on any tentative action plans that may have been previously discussed by the administration, such as those described in chapter 9.

Step 3: Solicit Requests from Employees for the Upcoming Year

A third step is to solicit purchase requests from employees for the upcoming year. Many of these requests are likely to be submitted by teachers, who might ask for items that include:

- Instructional supplies such as pencils, calculators, and science kits
- Books, magazines, and journals
- Subscriptions to online educational services and databases

- Classroom equipment such as dry erase boards and projectors
- Technology devices such as computers, printers, and smartboards
- Classroom furniture such as chairs, desks, and tables
- Field trips to specified venues
- Memberships to professional associations

Budget Request Form

In soliciting requests from employees, a standard budget request form should be used. Figure 11.1 is one possible version.

In this example, the top section of the form is used to identify the name of the employee making the request, their position, the building in which they work, and the name of their direct supervisor. It is also used to indicate whether the request pertains to technology and to identify the vendor from which the requested item(s) are to be purchased.

The middle section contains a table that is used to list product numbers, item descriptions, quantities, and prices. The table also includes columns to indicate whether the prices listed are estimates or exact amounts and to designate expense account(s) to which the items are to be charged. There is also a column to classify items as required or discretionary. Having this information helps to streamline the process of entering approved requests in the budget,

BUDGET REQUEST FORM:

Requester Name _____
Position _____
Building _____
Supervisor you report to _____

Technology request? Yes___ No___

Vendor Name _____
Address _____
Phone Number _____
Fax Number _____
Website _____
Email Address _____

Product Number	Item Description	Quantity	Unit Price	Total Cost	Estimate or Exact?	Expense Account	Required or Discretionary?

Requester Signature _____   Date _____   Subtotal _____
                                                                 Shipping _____
Approval 1:
Supervisor Signature _____   Date _____   Total _____

Approval 2:
Bus. Administrator Signature _____   Date _____

Approval 3:
Superintendent Signature _____   Date _____

Required if a Technology Request
Technology Director Signature _____   Date _____

Figure 11.1. Budget Request Form

and it also makes it easier to refine the budget and identify areas to cut later if necessary.

The bottom section contains lines to tally the cost of all items combined and to add shipping charges. It also contains signature and date lines for the requester and reviewers. In this case, the requester's immediate supervisor conducts the first level of review, followed by the business administrator and superintendent. The technology director's approval is also required for requests that have been marked as technology related. For example:

- Regular education teachers might report to a building principal.
- Special education teachers might report to a special education director.
- Maintenance technicians might report to a buildings and grounds director.
- Nurses and guidance counselors might report to a director of student support services.

The following modifications to the standard approval process might be made in a few special cases:

- Employees working in the business office might skip the first level of approval if their direct supervisor is the business administrator.
- Direct supervisors might sign off on their own requests on the first approval signature line.
- The superintendent might sign off on requests for their office before they are forwarded to the business office.

Keep in mind that figure 11.1 is a sample form that can be adjusted as needed to suit the needs of each individual school district; for instance, there may be different reviewers, more or fewer review layers, or a different order of review.

Budget Memo

When it is time to solicit budget requests, a memo should be sent to all employees explaining the purpose of the form, how to fill it out, and where and when to submit it. Assuming the budget request form in figure 11.1 is used, the memo might include the following instructions:

- Only one item per line can be listed.
- Product numbers and prices marked as exact must be based on the most current vendor catalogs and pricing information available.
- Books must be identified by ISBN.

- Requests from the same vendor must be shown on the same form or consecutive forms.
- All budget request forms must be submitted to the employee's direct supervisor by a specified date.
- All approved forms must be filled out entirely, signed by all required parties, and dated.
- All approved forms must be submitted to the business office by direct supervisors by a specified date.

In addition to spelling out all requirements, the memo should recommend that instructors teaching the same grade or subject collaborate to prevent unnecessary or duplicate requests. It may also be beneficial to explain the difference between certain types of expense accounts, such as those used to record the cost of supplies and those used to record the cost of equipment. Providing examples of technology items and describing the relationship between quantity, unit price, and total cost may also be helpful.

Step 4: Collect Approved Requests and Add to the Table

Requests that pass the first level of review should be forwarded by direct supervisors to the business office by the deadline specified in the memo so they can be reviewed further and recorded in the non-personnel budget table. In addition to making sure that the forms have been filled out in accordance with the instructions in the budget memo, some important questions to ask before entering the requests are:

- Have all costs been calculated correctly on each form, including those for individual line items, the subtotal, and total?
- Are the expense accounts that have been designated for each line item correct?
- Have items been classified as required or discretionary in a reasonable manner?

To verify that the expense accounts are correct, the account names should be compared to the items for which they have been designated. For instance, requested office supplies that have been assigned to a contracted service expense account have been coded incorrectly and should be recoded as necessary. In checking the classifications of items as required or discretionary, commonsense judgments can often be used. Requested supplies for a holiday party that have been marked as required, for example, should almost certainly be reclassified as discretionary.

Once the budget request forms have been checked and adjusted as needed, the items listed on the forms and associated details can be added to the non-personnel budget table. It is also possible that revisions to budgetary amounts entered in steps 1 and 2 will be necessary based on information from the forms. For instance, a budget estimate for a vehicle inspection that was already entered may need to be increased based on a request from the maintenance department for a major overhaul of the vehicle.

It is important to note that entering a request in the non-personnel budget table does not imply that it has been approved by the business administrator; it simply means that the request has been tentatively incorporated so that its financial effect is reflected in the overall budget projection.

Step 5: Calculate the Total Cost of All Items

Once all entries have been made in the table, the projected cost of all items combined should be calculated.

Step 6: Calculate the Budget for Each Expense Account

The final step is to calculate the budget for each expense account. Each account's budget should equal the total of all costs assigned to it in the table, and the total of all accounts combined should match the total from step 5. Categorizing the accounts by functional area, building, department, or other criteria and calculating the total budget for each group can also be helpful.

COLLABORATION AND SHARED PURPOSE

Completing the steps described above allows the subsidiary non-personnel budget table to be filled out, but for the information that has been entered to be of value, it needs to be accurate and complete. Because much of this information is directly from budget request forms submitted by employees, it is vital that they make a concerted effort when creating and/or reviewing budget requests. This requires a careful and deliberate comparison of resources they have on hand with their future needs that can serve as a sound basis for the requests they make. This approach helps to ensure that needed items are not overlooked while also helping to prevent wasteful spending requests.

To obtain employee buy-in, business administrators should take time to explain the purposes and applications of a school district budget, how it is generally developed, and the importance of budget accuracy. Employees should understand that budgeting is a collaborative effort and that the input they provide has a direct impact on the quality of the final product.

SMALL TOWN SCHOOL DISTRICT

Returning to Small Town School District, the finance director completes steps 1–3 and then, as part of step 4, collects those budget requests that have been approved by the other district administrators. The requests received are as follows, using the format "Item Description, Total Price, Estimate or Exact, Expense Account, Required or Discretionary":

Superintendent
- Membership dues for a professional association to which the superintendent belongs, $750, Exact, Central Office Dues and Fees, Required
- Registration fees for a specific conference, $500, Exact, Central Office Dues and Fees, Discretionary

Curriculum Director
- Curriculum mapping software license renewal, $300, Exact, Curriculum Software Expense, Required
- Defibrillator for high school nurse, $1,500, Exact, Nursing Supplies Expense, Required

Special Education Director
- Tuition for ten identified special education students at a specific school at a cost of $30,000 each, $300,000, Exact, Special Education Tuition, Required
- Screen-reading software for a special education student, $500, Exact, Learning Support Supplies Expense, Required

Buildings and Grounds Director
- Tractor, $25,000, Exact, Plant Equipment Expense, Discretionary
- New floor installations in three classrooms at a cost of $2,500 each, $7,500, Estimate, Building Repairs and Maintenance, Discretionary

Technology Director
- Device monitoring software renewal, $5,000, Exact, Technology Software Expense, Required
- Twenty-five new computers at a cost of $1,000 each, $25,000, Estimate, Technology Equipment Expense, Discretionary

High School Principal
- Three replacement books for science class at a cost of $120 each, $360, Exact, Regular Instruction Books Expense, Discretionary
- Repair of piano in music room, $1,000, Estimate, Regular Instruction Contracted Services, Discretionary

Elementary School Principal
- Field trip to local science center, $600, Estimate, Regular Instruction Field Trips, Discretionary

- Forty student workbooks for grade 3 at a cost of $20 each, $800, Exact, Regular Instruction Books Expense, Required

(Note that in an actual school district, there would likely be hundreds or even thousands of requests depending on the size of the district.)

Figure 11.2 represents Small Town School District's non-personnel budget table after completing steps 1–5.

As with the subsidiary personnel budget, estimated amounts that may still be adjusted are shown in italics.

Step 1

Some items listed in step 1 are contractually obligated or legally required, including the following:

- Building permit fees
- Alarm system monitoring agreement
- HVAC system preventive maintenance agreement
- Vehicle inspections
- Transportation agreement
- Bank loan payment
- Lease payments
- Financial audit

Of these, only the costs of vehicle inspections and contracted transportation services are estimates that may still be adjusted.

Other items listed are not necessarily legally required but are still considered to be essential, including the following:

- Financial software
- Insurance
- Legal retainer agreement

Of these, the projected costs of the financial software and legal retainer are known, while the projected cost of insurance is an estimate that is subject to change.

Estimates that are subject to change will be finalized later in the budgeting process, by either confirming that they are acceptable after additional analysis, refining them when more information becomes available, or converting them to exact amounts when actual quotes are received. For instance, the projected costs of vehicle inspections may be adjusted based on input from the buildings and grounds director, or the cost of contracted transportation

SUBSIDIARY NON-PERSONNEL BUDGET
Small Town School District

Item Description	Qty	Unit Price	Total Cost	Expense Account	Req/Discr	
Permit fees, ele school and high school	2	$ 100	$ 200	Building Inspections and Certificates	Req	
Alarm system monitoring agreement	12	$ 500	$ 6,000	Plant Contracted Services	Req	
HVAC system preventive maintenance agreement	4	$ 9,000	$ 36,000	Plant Contracted Services	Req	
Inspection, vehicle 1	1	$ 1,000	$ 1,000	Vehicle Inspections	Req	
Inspection, vehicle 2	1	$ 1,000	$ 1,000	Vehicle Inspections	Req	
Inspection, vehicle 3	1	$ 1,000	$ 1,000	Vehicle Inspections	Req	
Transportation agreement	1	$ 2,000,000	$ 2,000,000	Contracted Transportation Services	Req	Step 1. List Required Items and Details
Bank loan	1	$ 350,000	$ 350,000	Loan Payment	Req	
Postage machine lease	12	$ 400	$ 4,800	Lease Payments	Req	
Copier lease	12	$ 7,000	$ 84,000	Lease Payments	Req	
Financial software	1	$ 25,000	$ 25,000	Financial Software Expense	Req	
Financial audit	4	$ 5,000	$ 20,000	Audit Fees	Req	
Property insurance	1	$ 51,500	$ 51,500	District Insurance	Req	
Auto insurance	1	$ 5,150	$ 5,150	District Insurance	Req	
Cyber insurance	1	$ 15,450	$ 15,450	District Insurance	Req	
Legal retainer agreement	12	$ 1,000	$ 12,000	Legal Retainer	Req	
New building control system installation	1	$ 500,000	$ 500,000	Capital Projects	Discr	Step 2. Modify the List Based on Tentative Action Plans
Theater sound system upgrade	1	$ 30,000	$ 30,000	Capital Projects	Discr	
Security software and card readers installation	1	$ 15,000	$ 15,000	Capital Projects	Discr	
Membership dues	1	$ 750	$ 750	Central Office Dues and Fees	Req	Step 3. Solicit Requests from Employees for the Upcoming Year
Conference registration fee	1	$ 500	$ 500	Central Office Dues and Fees	Discr	
Curriculum mapping software renewal	1	$ 300	$ 300	Curriculum Software Expense	Req	
Defibrillator for high school nurse	1	$ 1,500	$ 1,500	Nursing Supplies Expense	Req	
Tuition for specific special education students	10	$ 30,000	$ 300,000	Special Education Tuition	Req	
Screen reading software	1	$ 500	$ 500	Learning Support Supplies Expense	Req	Step 4. Collect Approved Requests and Add to Table
Tractor	1	$ 25,000	$ 25,000	Plant Equipment Expense	Discr	
New floor installations	3	$ 2,500	$ 7,500	Building Repairs and Maintenance	Discr	
Device monitoring software renewal	1	$ 5,000	$ 5,000	Technology Software Expense	Req	
Computers	25	$ 1,000	$ 25,000	Technology Equipment Expense	Discr	
Replacement books for science class	3	$ 120	$ 360	Regular Instruction Books Expense	Discr	
Repair of piano in music room	1	$ 1,000	$ 1,000	Regular Instruction Contracted Services	Discr	
Field trip to local science center	1	$ 600	$ 600	Regular Instruction Field Trips	Discr	
Student workbooks for grade 3	40	$ 20	$ 800	Regular Instruction Books Expense	Req	

Step 5. Calculate the Total Cost of All Items → $ 3,526,910

Figure 11.2. Small Town School District Subsidiary Non-personnel Budget

may be updated based on a recommendation from the special education director (who also oversees transportation). The budgets for district insurance policies, which assume a 3 percent increase over current year costs based on recent historical trends, will be converted to exact amounts when quotes are received from insurance companies.

Step 2

The items listed in step 2 are from the administration's tentative action plans, described in chapter 9. All of these are classified as discretionary, and their costs are shown in italics since they are rough estimates that may be refined later.

Step 4

The items listed in step 4 are those requested by administrators on the forms they submitted. Four amounts are shown in italics to indicate that they are approximations that need to be reviewed further, and the administrators' classification of the items as required or discretionary are shown in the rightmost column of the table.

Step 5

The total cost of all items is calculated to be $3,526,910 in step 5. Because the total is a function of some items whose costs are known and others whose costs are estimates that may be adjusted later, the total is subject to change and is shown in italics to reflect this.

Step 6

The final step is to calculate the budget of each account by totaling the costs assigned to each in the table. The following are the results after completing this step, with the accounts categorized by functional area:

Regular Instruction
- Regular Instruction Books Expense: $360 + $800 = $1,160
- Regular Instruction Contracted Services: $1,000
- Regular Instruction Field Trips: $600
- Total: $2,760

Special Education
- Special Education Tuition: $300,000
- Learning Support Supplies Expense: $500

- Total: $300,500

Educational Administration
- Curriculum Software Expense: $300

Instructional Support Services
- Nursing Supplies Expense: $1,500

Ancillary Student Services
- Contracted Transportation Services: $2,000,000

Plant Operations
- Building Inspections and Certificates: $200
- Plant Contracted Services: $6,000 + $36,000 = $42,000
- Vehicle Inspections: $1,000 × 3 = $3,000
- Plant Equipment Expense: $25,000
- Building Repairs and Maintenance: $7,500
- Capital Projects: $500,000 + $30,000 + $15,000 = $545,000
- Total: $622,700

Business Operations
- Loan Payment: $350,000
- Lease Payments: $4,800 + $84,000 = $88,800
- Audit Fees: $20,000
- Financial Software Expense: $25,000
- District Insurance: $51,500 + $5,150 + 15,450 = $72,100
- Total: $555,900

Technology Operations
- Technology Software Expense: $5,000
- Technology Equipment Expense: $25,000
- Total: $30,000

Central and Board Operations
- Legal Retainer: $12,000
- Central Office Dues and Fees: $750 + $500 = $1,250
- Total: $13,250

The total of all accounts combined is $3,526,910, matching the amount calculated in step 5.

Chapter 12

Stage 4
Budget Miscellaneous Expenses and Add Contingency Allowance

The previous two chapters discussed the budgeting of personnel and non-personnel expenses that can be tied to specific employees or items. The recommendation was to project these expenses in subsidiary budgets and then to link them to accounts in the main expenditure budget.

EXAMPLES OF EXPENSES FOR MISCELLANEOUS EMPLOYEES OR ITEMS

Needless to say, not all projected expenses are associated with individuals, goods, or services that can be readily identified. Some can be associated only with miscellaneous employees or items. For instance, it is usually not possible to know exactly how overtime or substitute costs will be divided among a set of employees or which exact supplies will be purchased on an as-needed basis.

Conference Registration Fees and Travel Costs

Registration fees and travel costs for specific conferences that employees plan to attend in the upcoming year can be projected ahead of time in the subsidiary non-personnel budget, but these costs are also likely to result from miscellaneous conferences that employees attend throughout the year.

Repairs and Maintenance

The repair of equipment that is on a maintenance schedule for the upcoming year can be projected ahead of time, but these costs can also be incurred as a result of unexpected equipment malfunctions throughout the year.

Tuition and Educational Service Fees

School districts pay tuition when their students attend outside schools. In some cases, it may be known in advance that certain students will attend specific schools, but in others it is not possible to know in advance which students will attend and where they will be enrolled. For example, these costs may result from new students who move into the district and require specialized services at an outside institution or from existing students who decide to withdraw from the district and enroll in a charter school.

Tax Refunds

Tax refunds resulting from property assessment reductions or other factors may be required throughout the year. Knowing exactly which properties will be reassessed and the owners to whom the refunds will be owed is impossible to know ahead of time.

Legal Fees

Various legal expenses may come up throughout the year that are not covered under a retainer agreement.

BUDGETING EXPENSES FOR MISCELLANEOUS ITEMS

Expenses that are associated with miscellaneous employees or items should be projected directly in the main expenditure budget rather than the subsidiary budgets. As discussed in chapter 6, when an accounting software allows for pre-encumbrances, the budget for miscellaneous employees or items can be added to that for specific items in the same expense account without sacrificing control. This is because pre-encumbrances can be used to reduce the available balances of accounts to reflect planned orders and spending before they actually occur.

When a pre-encumbrance feature is not available, a different budgeting approach is needed to maintain the same level of control. This approach requires that expenses for miscellaneous employees or items be projected directly in the main expenditure budget under accounts separate from those linked to the subsidiary budget tables. For instance, if account "Building Principal Supplies Expense" is used to budget the cost of specific items requested by a building principal during the budget preparation period, a separate account such as "Miscellaneous Building Principal Supplies Expense" might be used to budget for various items they purchase throughout the year. When pre-encumbrances are not an option, it is recommended that there be at least one account for miscellaneous spending for each building, department, or functional area.

Budgeting expenses for miscellaneous items or employees often involves making estimates. Statistical techniques such as those presented in chapter 2 can be particularly helpful in making these estimates. For instance, if average annual spending on supplies for a building principal's office is $10,000, a decision may be made to budget this amount for their supplies in the upcoming year.

While the budgets for miscellaneous employees or items should be recorded in accounts separate from those used for specific items, the two should not be considered in isolation. If the building principal submits requests for $4,000 of specific items during the budget preparation period, for example, a decision may then be made to budget $6,000 for miscellaneous items so that the total budget remains at $10,000, in line with the historical results.

Steps for Budgeting Expenses for Miscellaneous Employees or Items

Step 1: Format the Main Expenditure Budget Table

Recall from chapter 6 that a recommended layout for the main expenditure budget table is to have separate columns for the names of expense accounts, historical charges to those accounts, statistical measures of the charges, and budget amounts. A first step in budgeting expenses for miscellaneous employees or items is to make sure the table is in the proper format before entering any data.

Step 2: List All Expense Accounts and Enter Historical Data and Statistical Measures

Once the main budget table is ready for use, the next step is to list all expense accounts in the "Account Names" column and their historical charges in adjacent columns. Statistical measures such as the historical mean, median, and linear regression forecast can then be determined and added in the other columns.

Step 3: Enter Budget Amounts for Expense Accounts Tied to Subsidiary Budgets

Next, the budget amounts for accounts that are tied to the subsidiary budgets should be entered. The main budget table may also be programmed to extract data from the subsidiary budget tables automatically.

Step 4: Determine and Enter Budget Amounts for Expense Accounts Designated for Miscellaneous Employees or Items

The fourth step is to determine and enter budget amounts for those accounts that are designated for miscellaneous employees or items.

Step 5: Calculate Total Budgeted Expenses for All Accounts and Add Contingency Allowance

Once all the account budgets are listed, the final step is to calculate the total budgeted expenses for all accounts and to add any required contingency allowance.

SMALL TOWN SCHOOL DISTRICT

Chapters 10 and 11 explained the processes Small Town School District used to develop its subsidiary personnel and non-personnel budgets and to calculate the budgets of accounts linked to them. Its process for budgeting expenses associated with miscellaneous employees or items will now be illustrated using the district's plant operations budget. While the discussion focuses primarily on this functional area, a similar set of steps can be applied to other functional areas as well.

Plant Operations Expenditure Budget

Figure 12.1 demonstrates what the plant operations expenditure budget looks like after applying preceding steps 1–4. The total budget for all accounts is also shown at the bottom of the figure.

The following are explanations pertaining to the amounts in the table.

Amounts Entered in Step 2

The amounts for years 1–5 are the historical charges to each account over the previous five years.

Stage 4

MAIN EXPENDITURE BUDGET
Small Town School District
Plant Operations Functional Area

Step 1. Format the Main Expenditure Budget Table

Account	Yr 1	Yr 2	Yr 3	Yr 4	Yr 5	Mean	Median	Yr 7 Regression Forecast	Yr 7 Budget
Plant salary, wage, and benefit accounts	$ 744,932	$ 763,555	$ 783,408	$ 804,560	$ 821,456	$ 783,582	$ 783,408	$ 861,203	$ 858,392
Building Inspections and Certificates	$ 190	$ 190	$ 195	$ 195	$ 200	$ 194	$ 195	$ 204	$ 200
Plant Contracted Services	$ 36,000	$ 36,000	$ 40,000	$ 42,000	$ 42,000	$ 39,200	$ 40,000	$ 46,400	$ 42,000
Vehicle Inspections	$ 2,494	$ 2,749	$ 2,866	$ 2,950	$ 2,785	$ 2,769	$ 2,785	$ 3,082	$ 3,000
Plant Equipment	$ 8,755	$ 13,819	$	$ 5,000	$	$ 5,515	$ 5,000	$ (5,017)	$ 25,000
Capital Projects	$ 216,921	$ 53,855	$ 846,700	$ 77,418	$ 126,724	$ 264,324	$ 126,724	$ 201,591	$ 545,000
Building Repairs and Maintenance	$ 5,250	$ 12,106	$ 6,709	$ 16,553	$ 9,871	$ 10,098	$ 9,871	$ 15,573	$ 7,500
Misc Building Repairs and Maintenance	$ 106,248	$ 93,127	$ 108,445	$ 104,727	$ 100,063	$ 102,522	$ 104,727	$ 102,214	$ 107,098
Custodial overtime and benefit accounts	$ 22,117	$ 26,746	$ 18,844	$ 18,055	$ 18,571	$ 20,867	$ 18,844	$ 14,553	$ 18,844
Misc Plant Travel	$ 513	$ 597	$ 388	$ 412	$ 478	$ 478	$ 478	$ 376	$ 478
Electricity	$ 186,025	$ 193,117	$ 204,033	$ 205,067	$ 207,619	$ 199,172	$ 204,033	$ 221,227	$ 221,227
Water and Sewage	$ 42,346	$ 44,866	$ 43,872	$ 45,334	$ 46,284	$ 44,540	$ 44,866	$ 47,878	$ 47,878
Natural Gas	$ 144,868	$ 147,611	$ 150,769	$ 160,131	$ 164,888	$ 153,653	$ 150,769	$ 174,677	$ 174,677
Misc Plant Supplies	$ 53,874	$ 50,063	$ 55,023	$ 17,071	$ 52,813	$ 45,769	$ 52,813	$ 31,723	$ 52,813
Misc Plant Dues and Fees	$ 18,325	$ 18,899	$ 19,353	$ 19,740	$ 20,135	$ 19,290	$ 19,353	$ 21,075	$ 21,075

Step 2. List All Expense Accounts and Enter Historical Data and Statistical Measures

Step 3. Enter Budget Amounts for Expense Accounts Tied to Subsidiary Budgets

Step 4. Determine and Enter Budget Amounts for Expense Accounts Designated for Miscellaneous Employees or Items

Total Plant Operations Expenditure Budget $ 2,125,182

Figure 12.1. Small Town School District Plant Operations Expenditure Budget

Amounts Entered in Step 3

The budget amounts entered in step 3 are calculated as follows using amounts from figures 10.1 and 11.2:

- Plant Salary, Wage, and Benefit Accounts ($858,392) = Buildings and grounds director ($114,662) + custodians 1–12 ($743,730)
- Building Inspections and Certificates ($200) = Permit fees, elementary school and high school ($200)
- Plant Contracted Services ($42,000) = Alarm system monitoring agreement ($6,000) + HVAC preventive maintenance agreement ($36,000)
- Vehicle Inspections ($3,000) = Inspection, vehicle 1 ($1,000) + inspection, vehicle 2 ($1,000) + inspection, vehicle 3 ($1,000)
- Plant Equipment ($25,000) = Tractor ($25,000)

- Capital Projects ($545,000) = New building control system installation ($500,000) + theater sound system upgrade ($30,000) + security software and card readers installation ($15,000)
- Building Repairs and Maintenance ($7,500) = New floor installations ($7,500)

Notice that the budgets for personnel costs, vehicle inspections, capital projects, and building repairs and maintenance are in italics because they are based on estimates that need to be reviewed further and possibly adjusted.

Amounts Entered in Step 4

The following are explanations of the budget amounts entered in step 4, all of which are shown in italics to indicate that they are not yet finalized:

- Misc Building Repairs and Maintenance ($107,098): The budget for this account is based on an analysis of historical costs for both planned and miscellaneous repairs and maintenance. Repairs and maintenance planned in advance are charged to the account "Building Repairs and Maintenance," while miscellaneous repairs and maintenance that are performed as they become necessary are charged to the account "Misc Building Repairs and Maintenance." The budget for the latter account ($107,098) has been set at the amount required to make the combined budget for both accounts match the historical median:

  Historical median charge to both accounts = $9,871 + $104,727 = $114,598

  Budget for both accounts = $7,500 + $107,098 = $114,598

  The historical median has been used as the basis for the projection since there is no clear upward or downward trend in the data.
- Custodial overtime and benefit accounts ($18,844): Here, too, the median serves as the basis for the budget projection. The data indicate that a change occurred in year 3 that reduced the cost of overtime and that this cost continued to be lower in the subsequent two years. The median has been selected because it is relatively close to the charges in years 3–5.
- Misc Plant Travel ($478): Here, the historical mean and median are the same, and they are used as the basis for the budget projection.
- Electricity ($221,227), Water and Sewage ($47,878), and Natural Gas ($174,677): The budgets for all three utilities are based on the regression forecast. This is because all are trending upward. Despite the decline in

the cost of water and sewage in year 3, there is still a general upward trend in this cost.
- Misc Plant Supplies ($52,813): The budget for plant supplies is based on the median. The mean was not chosen because it is skewed by the outlier in year 4, and the regression forecast was not used because there is no clear pattern in the data.
- Misc Plant Dues and Fees ($21,075): Dues and fees associated with the district's plant operations are increasing at a rate of about 2–3 percent per year, which is why the regression analysis is used as the basis for this account's budget.

Total Plant Operations Expenditure Budget

The total budget for all plant operations expense accounts combined is $2,125,182. Keep in mind that while these budget amounts are based on an analysis of the mean, median, and regression forecast, there is no rule stating that the budget must match one of these amounts. In many ways, budgeting is an art. When estimating future results, the goal should be to make one's best judgment based on experience, knowledge, and a scientific analysis of available data.

Other Functional Area Expenditure Budgets

Small Town School District uses a similar set of steps to develop budgets for its other functional areas and arrives at the following results.

Regular Instruction
- Expenses from subsidiary personnel budget = $9,036,319 (see chapter 10)
- Expenses from subsidiary non-personnel budget = $2,760 (see chapter 11)
- Expenses projected directly in the main budget for spending on miscellaneous employees or items = $947,000 (derived by completing steps 2–4 of chapter 12)
- Total Regular Instruction Expenditure Budget = $9,986,079

Special Education
- Expenses from subsidiary personnel budget = $1,673,618 (see chapter 10)
- Expenses from subsidiary non-personnel budget = $300,500 (see chapter 11)
- Expenses projected directly in the main budget for spending on miscellaneous employees or items (including tuition for students not specifically identified) = $1,916,825 (derived by completing steps 2–4 of chapter 12)
- Total Special Education Expenditure Budget = $3,890,943

Educational Administration
- Expenses from subsidiary personnel budget = $824,233 (see chapter 10)
- Expenses from subsidiary non-personnel budget = $300 (see chapter 11)
- Expenses projected directly in the main budget for spending on miscellaneous employees or items = $30,110 (derived by completing steps 2–4 of chapter 12)
- Total Educational Administration Expenditure Budget = $854,643

Instructional Support Services (Nursing and Guidance)
- Expenses from subsidiary personnel budget = $392,159 (see chapter 10)
- Expenses from subsidiary non-personnel budget = $1,500 (see chapter 11)
- Expenses projected directly in the main budget for spending on miscellaneous employees or items = $15,978 (derived by completing steps 2–4 of chapter 12)
- Total Instructional Support Services Expenditure Budget = $409,637

Ancillary Student Services (Transportation and Athletics)
- Expenses from subsidiary personnel budget = $14,130 (see chapter 10)
- Expenses from subsidiary non-personnel budget = $2,000,000 (see chapter 11)
- Expenses projected directly in the main budget for spending on miscellaneous employees or items = $140,000 (derived by completing steps 2–4 of chapter 12)
- Total Ancillary Student Services Expenditure Budget = $2,154,130

Business Operations
- Expenses from subsidiary personnel budget = $316,156 (see chapter 10)
- Expenses from subsidiary non-personnel budget = $555,900 (see chapter 11)
- Expenses projected directly in the main budget for spending on other miscellaneous employees or items (including tax refunds) = $10,980 (derived by completing steps 2–4 of chapter 12)
- Total Business Operations Expenditure Budget = $883,036

Technology Operations
- Expenses from subsidiary personnel budget = $164,122 (see chapter 10)
- Expenses from subsidiary non-personnel budget = $30,000 (see chapter 11)
- Expenses projected directly in the main budget for spending on miscellaneous employees or items = $85,000 (derived by completing steps 2–4 of chapter 12)
- Total Technology Operations Expenditure Budget = $279,122

Central and Board Operations
- Expenses from subsidiary personnel budget = $266,241 (see chapter 10)

- Expenses from subsidiary non-personnel budget = $13,250 (see chapter 11)
- Expenses projected directly in the main budget for spending on miscellaneous employees or items (including those for legal services falling outside retainer agreement and public relations and advertising) = $80,165 (derived by completing steps 2–4 of chapter 12)
- Total Central and Board Operations Expenditure Budget = $359,656

Calculate Total Budgeted Expenses for All Accounts and Add Contingency Allowance

The total projected expenses for the entire budget are then calculated by adding the budgets for each functional area:

Regular Instruction: $9,986,079
Special Education: $3,890,943
Educational Administration: $854,643
Instructional Support Services: $409,637
Ancillary Student Services: $2,154,130
Plant Operations: $2,125,182
Business Operations: $883,036
Technology Operations: $279,122
Central and Board Operations: $359,656
Total Budgeted Expenses: $20,942,428

A final step is to add the board's required contingency allowance of 1 percent from chapter 9:

Total Budgeted Expenses: $20,942,428
Contingency Allowance: $20,942,428 × 0.01 = $209,424
Total Budgeted Expenses + Contingency
Allowance = $20,942,428 + $209,424
= $21,151,852

Chapter 13

Stage 5
Budget Revenues

In addition to expense projections, a budget consists of revenue projections. While the preceding three chapters focused on the development of the expenditure budget, the focus of this chapter is the revenue budget. Before demonstrating how Small Town School District develops its revenue budget, a review of some of the concepts presented in chapter 5 regarding local revenues is instructive.

Recall that school districts receive revenues from local, state, and federal sources. Local revenues are generated primarily by taxes, with property taxes being most significant. The total property tax that a school district charges in a given year is the sum of the taxes charged against all properties in the district, as represented in the following formula:

Total Property Tax Charged on All Properties = Total Assessment of All Properties × Property Tax Rate (mills) × 0.001

Not all tax bills are paid, so to calculate the actual taxes collected (tax revenue), the preceding amount is adjusted based on the collection percentage:

Property Tax Revenue = Total Property Tax Charged on All Properties × Collection Percentage

The amount to budget for property tax revenue is then:

Estimated Property Tax Revenue = Total Assessment of All Properties × Property Tax Rate (mills) × 0.001 × Estimated Collection Percentage

If property tax calculations for the upcoming year will be based on property assessments on a future date (e.g., the date on which tax bills will be sent), the total assessment will have to be estimated as well.

In some instances, school districts may impose other taxes such as income or sales tax. These taxes can be budgeted in a manner similar to that just described for property tax using the following formulas:

Estimated Income Tax Revenue = Estimated Total Income of All Taxpayers × Income Tax Rate × Estimated Collection Percentage
Estimated Sales Tax Revenue = Estimated Total Sales × Sales Tax Rate × Estimated Collection Percentage

As an alternative, a simpler approach is just to base the budget amounts on the total revenue generated by each tax in prior years.

Another form of local revenue is investment income. School district investment income is usually in the form of interest, and the formula to calculate interest over a period of one year is as follows, assuming no further investments or withdrawals occur during the year:

Interest Income = Amount Invested at Beginning of Year × Effective Interest Rate

STEPS FOR COMPLETING THE REVENUE BUDGET

The procedures for completing the revenue budget are quite simple. The first step is to determine an appropriate budget for each revenue account, and the second is to calculate the total budget for all accounts.

SMALL TOWN SCHOOL DISTRICT

The previous three chapters discussed the development of Small Town School District's expenditure budget. The development of its revenue budget is now the focus.

Step 1: Determine an Appropriate Budget for Each Revenue Account

As indicated in chapter 8, Small Town School District has several sources of local revenue, including local taxes, investment income, rental proceeds, and admission and website advertising fees.

Property Tax Revenue

To budget property tax revenue, the district begins with the following formula:

Estimated Property Tax Revenue = Total Assessment of All Properties × Property Tax Rate (mills) × 0.001 × Estimated Collection Percentage

Recall that the district's property tax rate is 21.4 mills and that the total assessment of all properties is currently $642,386,121. There is also a new commercial development in progress that is expected to add $10,000,000 to the overall assessment by the beginning of the upcoming year, when the tax bills will be calculated based on assessments at that time. Applying this information and the district's typical collection rate of 95 percent as an estimated rate for the upcoming year, the budget for property tax revenue is calculated as follows:

Estimated Property Tax Revenue = ($642,386,121
+ $10,000,000) × 21.4 × 0.001 × 0.95
= $13,263,010

Further recall that the district's delinquent property tax collections have typically been between 3 and 7 percent of current collections. Using a middle value of 5 percent for the estimate, the budget for delinquent property taxes is calculated to be:

Estimated Delinquent Property Tax Revenue =
Estimated Property Tax Revenue × 0.05
$13,263,010 × 0.05
= $663,150

A more involved analysis might consider other factors as well, such as delinquent tax collection trends, the economic outlook for the upcoming year, and the remaining delinquent balance of all properties combined.

Income Tax Revenue

As previously noted, Small Town School District's income tax revenues have been as follows over the past five years:

- 5 years ago: $1,660,299
- 4 years ago: $1,716,713
- 3 years ago: $1,810,542
- 2 years ago: $1,927,475
- 1 year ago: $2,027,472

The annual increases are quite consistent, so conducting a linear regression analysis of the historical data is a reasonable and straightforward way to forecast future income tax revenues. The linear regression formula turns out to be:

$$\text{Income Tax Revenue} = \$94{,}511 \times \text{Year} + \$1{,}545{,}000$$

This yields an estimate of $2,206,577 for year 7. A budget amount of $2,206,500 is chosen based on the results of the regression analysis.

Investment Income

Small Town School District believes its savings account balance will still be at about $2,000,000 at the start of the upcoming year. Since the account provides an effective interest rate of 3.25 percent and the rate is expected to remain steady, the interest income it will generate can be estimated as follows for budgeting purposes:

$$\text{Estimated Interest Income} = \text{Estimated Amount Invested} \times \text{Estimated Interest Rate}$$
$$\$2{,}000{,}000 \times 0.0325 = \$65{,}000$$

Admission Fees, Rental Proceeds, and Website Advertising Fees

Based on amounts generated in the past, Small Town School District budgets the following amounts for admission fees and rental proceeds:

- Admission Fees: $30,000
- Rental Proceeds: $17,000

Website advertising fees of $19,300 are budgeted based on the increasing trend in those fees.

State and Federal Revenue Accounts

The amounts budgeted for state revenues are based on recommendations from the professional school business association to which the district belongs, which, as noted in chapter 8, are:

- Basic Education Subsidy: $3,290,000
- Special Education Subsidy: $712,500
- Student Transportation Services Subsidy: $436,000
- Student Health Services Subsidy: $18,745

Recall that the district also receives an annual Title I award that is used to pay for one teacher's salary and benefits. The amount budgeted for Title I revenue is set to match the total personnel costs associated with the Title I teacher in Figure 10.1, which are $102,947. This is slightly less than the federal grants manager's estimation of $104,000.

Step 2. Calculate Total Budget for All Revenue Accounts

Small Town School District calculates its total budgeted revenues for all accounts to be $20,824,152, as shown:

Local Revenue
- Property Tax Revenue: $13,263,010
- Delinquent Property Tax Revenue: $663,150
- Income Tax Revenue: $2,206,500
- Investment Income: $65,000
- Admission Fees: $30,000
- Rental Proceeds: $17,000
- Website Advertising Fees: $19,300
- Total Local Revenue: $16,263,960

State Revenue
- Basic Education Subsidy: $3,290,000
- Special Education Subsidy: $712,500
- Student Transportation Services Subsidy: $436,000
- Student Health Services Subsidy: $18,745

- Total State Revenue: $4,457,245

Federal Revenue
- Title I Grant Revenue: $102,947
- Total Revenue: $20,824,152

Chapter 14

Stage 6
Meet, Make Adjustments, and Finalize Budget

Chapters 10–13 discussed the development of draft revenue and expenditure budgets. Two types of expense accounts were considered: those with budgets based on the projected costs of specific employees or items in the subsidiary budgets and those with budgets for spending that cannot be tied to specific sources. The addition of a contingency allowance to the expenditure budget was also discussed.

SHARE BUDGET INFORMATION WITH ADMINISTRATORS

Once the draft budgets are complete, administrators (or the employees responsible for overseeing accounts within those budgets) should be provided with custom reports showing the budgets of accounts they oversee and any underlying line items from the subsidiary budgets so they can be reviewed.

Personnel Budget Report

A personnel budget report should be provided to each administrator listing the positions and employees they oversee and the number of days and hours budgeted for each wage position. The priority classification of each position (i.e., whether it is labeled as essential or expendable) should be included in the report, and estimates that may still be adjusted should be clearly labeled. Unless an administrator oversees accounts used to track personnel expenses or is involved in human resources or payroll functions, in most cases the report does not need to include the compensation and benefits of individual employees. A suggested format for the personnel budget report is as follows:

- Column 1: Position
- Column 2: Employee Name
- Column 3: Annual Days (wage employees only)
- Column 4: Hours per Day (wage employees only)
- Column 5: Priority Classification (essential or expendable)

Non-Personnel Budget Reports

In addition to the personnel budget report, each administrator should be provided with a non-personnel budget report showing all items in the non-personnel budget charged to accounts they oversee in the main budget. These reports should provide details such as item quantities, prices, and the expense accounts to which the items have been budgeted. The following is a recommended format for this report:

- Column 1: Item Description
- Column 2: Quantity
- Column 3: Unit Price
- Column 4: Budgeted Cost
- Column 5: Precision of Budgetary Amount (estimate that may still be adjusted, finalized estimate, or exact)
- Column 6: Expense Account Charged
- Column 7: Priority Classification (required or discretionary)

Main Budget Reports

Finally, a report should be provided to each administrator listing all revenue and expense accounts they oversee and the historical charges and budgets for each. This information, combined with that from the personnel and non-personnel budget reports, should allow the administrators to evaluate their account budgets and determine whether or not they feel that any adjustments are warranted.

Sample Reports

The following are sample reports that might be provided to a special education director who among their other duties oversees a federal IDEA grant of $10,000 that is used to pay for supplies:

Personnel Budget Report
- Learning Support Teacher, Sandra Jackson, Essential
- Learning Support Aide # 1, Elizabeth Schmidt, 184 days per year, 7 hours per day, Essential
- Learning Support Aide # 2, Jacob Wiley, 184 days per year, 6.5 hours per day, Essential
- Life Skills Teacher # 1, Judy Coll, Essential
- Life Skills Teacher # 2, Mark Lyle, Essential

Non-Personnel Budget Report
- Widget A, Quantity 2, Unit Price $200, Budgeted Cost $400, Exact, Learning Support Supplies, Required
- Widget B, Quantity 5, Unit Price $160, Budgeted Cost $800, Estimate that may still be adjusted, Life Skills Supplies, Discretionary
- Widget C, Quantity 1, Unit Price $500, Budgeted Cost $500, Exact, IDEA Grant Supplies, Required

Main Budget Report
- IDEA Grant Revenues, Charges in each of last five years, Budget $10,000
- Learning Support Supplies, Charges in each of last five years, Budget $400
- Miscellaneous Learning Support Supplies, Charges in each of last five years, Budget $5,000
- Life Skills Supplies, Charges in each of last five years, Budget $800
- Miscellaneous Life Skills Supplies, Charges in each of last five years, Budget $3,000
- IDEA Grant Supplies, Charges in each of last five years, Budget $500
- Miscellaneous IDEA Grant Supplies, Charges in each of last five years, Budget $9,500

Notice that the total revenues and total expenses for the IDEA grant match as required.

MEET WITH ADMINISTRATORS

Once the administrators have had a chance to review their budget reports, one or more meetings should be scheduled to discuss their findings and recommendations. These meetings can be conducted with each administrator separately or with all the administrators as a group. Individual meetings are appropriate when focusing on specific areas of the budget, while group meetings are more suitable when collaborating and coordinating plans for multiple areas. For example, principals from two elementary schools might compare the curriculum materials their teachers have requested to make sure they align. Budget meetings might include a superintendent who guides the discussion, a business administrator who primarily focuses on costs and financial goals, educational administrators who champion student needs, and other administrators who advocate for resources they feel are needed.

Group meetings tend to produce better results when there is open dialogue and debate. When meeting participants feel comfortable making suggestions, asking questions, and challenging one another, innovative thinking can flourish.

Go Over Needed Corrections

One purpose of the budget meetings is to go over any needed corrections that might be necessary as a result of errors that have been identified or new information that has come to light. The following sections provide a few examples of possible corrections.

Items That Need to Be Added

Some items may need to be added to the budget, such as:

- An employee who was inadvertently missed
- A special education student who just enrolled in an outside school
- A professional membership fee that was overlooked
- A software product an administrator forgot to include in their budget requests
- New revenue and expense accounts to track financial information for a grant that recently became available

Items That Need to Be Removed

Throughout the year, a school district business office receives numerous invoices, some of which provide information that is pertinent to the subsequent year's budget. For example, if a bill for a software license covering one year is received, the cost of the license should likely be budgeted for the following year. The budget meetings provide an opportunity to review those costs that have been tentatively budgeted based on information gleaned from invoices in order to determine whether any can be removed. The following are a few examples:

- A district receives monthly tuition bills for a special education student to attend an outside school. Based on this, the cost of their tuition is tentatively budgeted for the following year. The district's special education

director indicates that this cost can be removed from the budget because the student will return to the district in the following year.
- A technology director points out that the cost of an individual classroom license that has been budgeted for a certain educational software is unnecessary because it duplicates a districtwide license that has been included in their budget requests.
- A principal advises that the cost of a contracted service they purchased for the current year can be removed from the budget because they are not satisfied with the service and plan to discontinue it.

Coding and Other Errors

Administrators may also bring up coding or other errors they have identified. For example, a life skills teacher may have been mistakenly classified as a learning support teacher, or an aide who works seven hours per day has been budgeted for only 6.5 hours.

Go Over Suggested Revisions to Estimates

In addition to identifying needed corrections, administrators may also suggest revisions to budgetary amounts that have been labeled as estimates that may still be adjusted. This may be because they feel the estimates should be different based on their own judgment, or it may be that they know what the actual amount will be. For example, a facilities director might suggest increasing the amount budgeted for custodial overtime due to anticipated staffing shortages, or a principal may argue that their budget for miscellaneous supplies is too low based on historical spending. Some other possible suggestions are changes to the amounts budgeted for:

- Field trips
- Vehicle inspections
- Repairs and maintenance
- Utilities
- Revenues from grants for which official award letters were recently received

Administrators should be able to explain the reasoning behind any revisions they recommend. As an example, a special education director who suggests that additional funds should be budgeted for field trips for life skills students might argue that it is important to give these students more real-world experiences and tie their argument to a district's educational goals.

Adjust Plans

The budget meetings also present an opportunity to revisit any tentative action plans that may have been previously discussed (such as those outlined in chapter 9) and hash out any details that remained. For instance, the estimated cost of a plan to install smartboards in each classroom may now be refined in the budget if a specific brand has been selected.

ADJUST THE BUDGET

Once all budget meetings have taken place, the next step is to adjust the budget to account for any changes that were discussed and approved. It is important to keep in mind that any changes to grant revenue budgets must be accompanied by matching changes to their expenditure budgets to keep them in balance.

While the budget meetings may lead to the adjustment of budgetary estimates, it is likely that there will be some estimates that are still not finalized following the meetings; for example:

- The budgeted compensation and benefits for a vacant position may still not be finalized because a new person has not yet been chosen to fill it.
- The budget for employee pension costs may still not be finalized because the state pension system has not certified the rate for the upcoming year yet.
- Estimated health insurance premiums may still be subject to change because employees have not yet made their coverage selections for the upcoming year.
- Budgeted premiums for district insurance (i.e., property, auto, cyber, etc.) may still be tentative because quotes from insurance companies have not yet been received.

Estimates that will be revised based on information that is obtained outside the budget meetings should be adjusted as the information becomes available.

COMPARE PROJECTED NET RESULT TO REQUIREMENT

Once all required adjustments to the budget have been made, the next step is to calculate the budget's projected net result:

Projected Net Result = Budgeted Revenues − (Budgeted Expenses + Contingency Allowance)

This should then be compared to the desired result to determine whether any further adjustments are needed. For example, if the desired result is a deficit of no more than $100,000 and the budget projects a deficit of $150,000 (i.e., the projected net result is −$150,000), the projected result is not acceptable and must be improved by reducing the deficit by $50,000.

In order to improve a projected result, plans must be adjusted to increase projected revenues and/or reduce projected expenses. In the example provided above, if projected revenues can somehow be increased by $50,000, the desired result will be achieved. Determining the required reduction in budgeted expenses is slightly more complex if a contingency allowance that is a percentage of those expenses is required. The formula to calculate the necessary reduction is as follows, assuming there are no adjustments to revenues:

Required Reduction in Budgeted Expenses = Amount by Which the Projected Result Must be Improved / (1 + Contingency Allowance)

If in the preceding example a contingency allowance that is 1.50 percent of budgeted expenses has been stipulated and factored into the budget projection, the required reduction in budgeted expenses is $49,261:

Required Reduction in Budgeted Expenses = $50,000 / (1 + 0.015)
= $50,000 / 1.015
= $49,261

DETERMINE FURTHER ADJUSTMENTS TO MAKE

If a comparison of the projected net result to the desired result does indeed indicate that further adjustments are needed, additional administrative meetings may be necessary to look for ways to generate additional revenues, scale back plans, streamline operations, and/or cut waste. Some possible ideas may include:

- Cutting positions that are considered expendable
- Cutting programs that are not part of the core curriculum, such as arts and athletics programs
- Scaling back or eliminatng planned capital projects
- Using cheaper suppliers

- Trimming planned spending on conferences and travel
- Reducing the budget for discretionary supplies
- Applying for more grants

Before diving too far into the discussion, the team should come to a consensus on the importance of items that have been included in the budget. In other words, there should be general agreement on which positions and employees are essential or expendable and which non-personnel items are required or discretionary.

Reaching a consensus may be challenging if team members have opposing values and strong disagreements about the importance of certain items. Ideally, the conversation should be a lively but civil debate, with each person advocating their positions and tying their arguments to the district's values and strategic goals. The following are a few examples of cuts that might be under consideration and possible counterarguments.

- Cuts to Teaching Staff—A counterargument might be that the quality of instruction and educational outcomes will decline as a result of:
  - Increased class sizes
  - Fewer elective offerings for students
  - Greater course loads and reduced prep time for teachers
  - Teacher burnout and disgruntlement
- Cuts to Athletic Programs—Counterarguments might be that:
  - Athletic programs promote student health and fitness
  - Participation in sports teaches teamwork and leadership skills
  - School spirit will decline
- Elimination of School Library—Counterarguments might be that:
  - School libraries provide important resources for student research projects
  - School libraries promote reading
  - School libraries reduce educational inequities
- Elimination of One-to-One Technology Device Program—Counterarguments might be that:
  - Providing each student with their own device encourages engagement in learning
  - A one-to-one program helps to provide equal access to technology
  - A one-to-one program increases opportunities for differentiated instruction

If it turns out that not enough adjustments can be identified to make up the gap between the projected and desired results, it may be necessary to recommend a tax increase as part of the overall budget that is presented to the school board for consideration. If this is still not enough to make up the difference, it may be necessary for the board to reconsider the strategic goals and financial parameters it has set.

PRESENTING THE BUDGET AND COMPLETING REMAINING TASKS

Once the projected financial result is satisfactory, the budget can be presented to various stakeholders such as the school board, community, and district employees. This may be done through one or more formal presentations or by simply making the budget available for review, depending on the practice at each individual school district. The budget can then be passed by the board and submitted to any state or other regulatory agencies required, assuming there are no major objections to doing so.

Once the budget is passed, any remaining signatures required for those requests that were included in the final budget should be obtained. In addition, "not yet finalized" designations can be removed from the final versions of the subsidiary and main budgets.

SMALL TOWN SCHOOL DISTRICT

To demonstrate how Small Town School District applies the procedures discussed in this chapter, a simplifying assumption will first be made that budget reports have already been provided to each administrator, initial meetings have taken place, and no adjustments have been recommended. With this in mind, it is now possible to compare the budget's projected net result to the desired result.

Recall from chapters 12 and 13 that total budgeted revenue was $20,824,152, while the total of budgeted expenses and the 1 percent contingency allowance was $21,151,852. The projected net result is then a deficit of $327,700:

$$\text{Projected Net Result} = \text{Budgeted Revenues} - (\text{Budgeted Expenses} + \text{Contingency Allowance})$$
$$= \$20,824,152 - \$21,151,852$$
$$= -\$327,700$$

Because the board requirement was a balanced budget, the amount by which the projected result must be improved is $327,700. To accomplish this, plans must be adjusted to increase projected revenues and/or reduce projected expenses.

The administrative team meets again to try to identify adjustments that can be made and first considers ways to increase projected revenues. Unable to identify any feasible ways to increase revenues outside of a tax increase, the team then turns its attention to expenses. Because projected revenues will remain the same, it must try to find ways to reduce budgeted expenses by $324,455, calculated as follows:

Required Reduction in Budgeted Expenses = Amount by Which Projected Result Must be Improved / (1 + Contingency Allowance)
= $327,700 / (1 + 0.01)
= $327,700 / 1.01
= $324,455

Based on Small Town School District's subsidiary expenditure budgets developed in chapters 10 and 11, the team can consider cutting or eliminating the following:

- Positions Labeled as Expendable in Subsidiary Personnel Budget (Figure 10.1):
  - New math teacher: $83,032
  - New math tutor: $15,230
- Items Labeled as Discretionary in Subsidiary Non-Personnel Budget (Figure 11.2):
  - New building control system installation: $500,000
  - Theater sound system upgrade: $30,000
  - Computers: $25,000
  - Tractor: $25,000
  - Security software and card readers installation: $15,000
  - New floor installations: $7,500
  - Repair of piano in music room: $1,000
  - Field trip to local science center: $600
  - Conference registration fee: $500
  - Replacement books for science class: $360

Trimming the budgets of accounts for miscellaneous employees or items in the main expenditure budget may also be considered as a way to reduce projected expenses. From chapter 12, this includes the following accounts related to the district's plant operations:

- Electricity: $221,227
- Natural Gas: $174,677
- Misc Building Repairs and Maintenance: $107,098

- Misc Plant Supplies: $52,813
- Water and Sewage: $47,878
- Misc Plant Dues and Fees: $21,075
- Custodial overtime and benefit accounts: $18,844
- Misc Plant Travel: $478

It also includes accounts from the following functional areas that add up to the amount shown for each:

- Regular Instruction: $947,000
- Special Education: $1,916,825
- Educational Administration: $30,110
- Instructional Support Services: $15,978
- Ancillary Student Services: $140,000
- Business Operations: $10,980
- Technology Operations: $85,000
- Central and Board Operations: $80,165

The total of the amounts listed from all three budgets is $4,573,370. The team must try to identify enough ways to cut these projected expenses by 7.1 percent ($324,455 / $4,573,370). If it is unable to do so, one other option is to recommend a tax increase. The board previously indicated a willingness to consider a property tax increase of up to 2 percent (see chapter 9), which would take the rate from 21.4 mills to 21.828 mills. Because budgeted property tax revenues were $13,263,010 (see chapter 13), raising the tax rate by 2 percent would bring in approximately $265,260 more in property tax revenue:

$$\$13{,}263{,}010 \times 0.02 = \$265{,}260$$

This would reduce the amount by which the administrative team must cut budgeted expenses to a more manageable level.

Index

Page references for figures are italicized.

access control system. *See* security
administration and management:
business administration, 24–25,
77; central office administration
and role of superintendent, 25;
educational administration, 18,
49; grants administration, 18–19;
plant operations supervision, 23;
public relations, 26; technology
management, 24
ancillary student services:
extracurricular activities, 19; food
service, 20; student transportation, 20
assessment function, 6–7;
benchmarking, 6, 72; interpreting
budget variances, 6

board of directors, 25–26
budget accuracy: how to achieve, 3;
importance of, 1, 3–7
budget definition, 1
budgeting: adjustments to budget
in order to satisfy requirements,
2–3, 118–21; challenges of, 16,
71; of contracted services, 35;
of contractual and other required
items, 85–86; corrections examples,
116–17; of grants, 19; of insurance,
78; of loans and leases, 34–35; of
miscellaneous expenses, 98–100;
ongoing nature of, 57–58; presenting
and finalizing the budget, 121;
revisions and refinements, 117;
stages of, 58; styles of, 3
budget reports for administrators and
managers, 113–15
budget requests, soliciting, 86–89;
budget memo, 88–89; budget request
form, 87–88
buildings, 21

collaborative nature of budgeting, 58,
90; meeting with administrators
and prioritizing items, 120;
stakeholders, 71, 121
collective bargaining agreement, 29
compensation. *See* employee
compensation
construction projects: bond issuances
for, 21; construction managers, 21;
costs of, 21
consumable supplies, examples of, 35
control function, 5; making spending
decisions using pre-encumbrances,

125

49–50, 98; modifying account structure for better control when pre-encumbrances are not available, 50–52, 98–99

deficit, effect on financial position, 1
discretionary items in example household budget, 3

Elementary and Secondary School Emergency Relief Fund, 42
employee compensation: budgeting of, 31, 77–78; overtime, 26, 32; salaries and wages, 26, 29
employee pensions, 27, 33; budgeting of, 78
estimated budget amounts: examples of, 2–3, 35–36, 38, 39, 79; refining in subsidiary non-personnel budget, *93*
exact budget amounts, examples, 2, 35, 39
expenditure budget, 29; expense account designations, 50–52, 54; layout of, 45–49, *52*; ledger maintenance, 51–52

Federal Emergency Management Agency, 42
federal revenue, 41–42
FICA (Social Security and Medicare), 27; budgeting of, 32–33
financial audit, 25
financial position and relation to revenues and expenses, 1

health insurance, 33–34; factors that affect premiums and how they are paid, 27; hypothetical coverage levels and premiums, 64

instructional support services, 17–18
intrusion detection system. *See* security

laws and regulations: American Recovery and Reinvestment Act, 42; American Rescue Plan Act of 2021, 42; Civil Rights Act of 1964, 16, 25; Coronavirus Aid, Relief, and Economic Security Act of 2020, 42; Coronavirus Response and Relief Supplemental Appropriations Act of 2021, 42; Elementary and Secondary Education Act of 1965, 41; Fair Labor Standards Act, 26; Individuals with Disabilities Education Act (IDEA) of 1997, 16, 42; purchasing laws, 28
leases, example of equipment that might be leased, 28
legal fee structure, 26
linking subsidiary budgets to main expenditure budget, 53–54
local revenue: income tax and budgeting of, 39, 108; interest/investment income, 39, 66, 108; local grants, 39; other local revenues, 40; property tax and budgeting of, 37–38, 107–8; sales tax and budgeting of, 39, 108; tax collection percentage, 38, 107–8

Medicare. *See* FICA (Social Security and Medicare)
mill, definition of, 37
miscellaneous expenses: budgeting procedures for, 98–100; examples of, 53, 97–98
miscellaneous vs. planned spending, 49–52

non-personnel expenses: account categories used to track, 45–46; examples of, 36

personnel accounts, examples of, 45–46
personnel expenses, 26, 29, 77
planning function, 1–4, 73; cutting expenses, possible ideas, 119–20; establishing strategic goals and parameters, 72; factoring for contingency allowance when

determining required budget adjustments, 118–19; making budget adjustments to satisfy requirements, 2–3, 118–21; meeting with administrators to make budget adjustments, 115–18; tax increase consideration, 120
plant operations: contracted services, 22; inspections and tests of building equipment, 22–23; equipment maintained by, 21–22; facilities management service, 22; grounds maintenance, 22; replacements and renovations, 23; supplies used by, 22
prioritizing spending items, 53, 72–73, 79, 120
professional development and travel costs, 28
professional school business associations, 41
property assessments, 37–38, 107–8

required items in example household budget, 2–3
revenue budget layout, 55–56
revenue sources, 37
risk management: contingency allowance, 7, 72; financial audit, 25; insurance, 25, 35–36; internal controls, 25

salary schedules, 29–31
school board. *See* board of directors
security, 23
Small Town School District: accounting system, 67–69; administration, 63; alarm system components and monitoring agreement, 61; ancillary services, 62–63; budget adjustment required, 122; budget requests, 91–92; buildings and equipment, 61–62; contingency allowance, 74; contracted building and security services, 61; delinquent tax collections, 66; development of goals, parameters, and plans, 73–76; educational programs and student support services, 62; employee benefits, 64–65; grant budget, 115; grants, 67; insurance, 65; legal and accounting services, 65; loans and leases, 65; main expenditure budget, plant operations functional area, 100; plant operations, 62; property tax rate, 66; regression analysis, 110; revenues, 66–67; software, 65; state subsidies, 67; steps used to budget expenses for miscellaneous employees or items, 100–105; steps used to complete revenue budget, 108–12; steps used to complete subsidiary non-personnel budget, 91–95; steps used to complete subsidiary personnel budget, 79–84; steps used to meet, make adjustments and cuts, and finalize budget, 121–23; subsidiary non-personnel budget, *93*; subsidiary personnel budget, *80*; tax increase option and effect, 123; values, 61, 74
Social Security. *See* FICA (Social Security and Medicare)
special education, 15–16; assistive devices for special education students, 16; English language learners, 16, 40; functional areas, 48
state subsidies, grants, and funding formulas, 40–41
statistical measures and methods: average annual change method, 10–11; average percentage change method, 11; data trends, 10–14; mean, 9; median, 10; regression analyses, 12–14; use of to minimize budget variances, 9
student support services. *See* instructional support services
subsidiary non-personnel budget: entering data in, 89–90; examples of expenses to include in, 54; examples

of notes to record in on ongoing basis, *58*; layout of, 54, 55; steps for developing, 85–90

subsidiary personnel budget, 53–54; calling attention to and refining estimates in process, 79; examples of expenses tied to specific employees to project in, 53; examples of notes to record in on ongoing basis, *59*; steps for developing, 77–79

supply and equipment costs, 28

surplus, effect on financial position, 1

technology network, 24

Title grants, 41, 62, 67

unemployment compensation insurance, 27; budgeting, 34, 78

unions, 29. *See also* collective bargaining agreement

US Department of Education Office for Civil Rights, 16

US Department of Labor, 26

workers' compensation insurance, 27, 34

About the Author

Christopher Ursu has been employed as a school district business official for thirteen years and previously worked as a finance director at a nonprofit organization and adjunct faculty member at the University of Pittsburgh College of Business Administration. He is a member of the Association of School Business Officials and the Pennsylvania Association of School Business Officials and has had articles published by both organizations.

Chris received a BS from Grove City College and an MBA from the University of Pittsburgh Joseph M. Katz Graduate School of Business. He lives in Pittsburgh, Pennsylvania, with his wife, their two children, and their cat.

www.ingramcontent.com/pod-product-compliance
Lightning Source LLC
Chambersburg PA
CBHW032028230426
43671CB00005B/237